AT HOME WITH
ILLINOIS GOVERNORS

A Social History of the Illinois Executive Mansion

1855 – 2003

Lura Lynn Ryan observing the artist at work on a painting in the garden.

AT HOME WITH
ILLINOIS GOVERNORS

A Social History of the Illinois Executive Mansion
1855 – 2003

By: Dan Monroe,
with Lura Lynn Ryan, First Lady of Illinois 1999-2003

Featuring Watercolors by: Kay Smith

The genesis of this book was a conversation I had with John Trutter, author of a book on John Tanner, governor of Illinois from 1897-1901, and his wife Cora English Tanner. The Tanners sponsored a renovation of the Executive Mansion at the turn of the century. I learned that there was no written history of this magnificent building, the home of Illinois' governors since 1855.

The third oldest governor's mansion in the United States, the Illinois Executive Mansion has been the setting for great events. Abraham Lincoln called often as he counseled Governor William H. Bissell in the fateful years preceding the Civil War. American presidents from Ulysses S. Grant to George W. Bush have visited here to commune with Illinois governors and political figures. The Mansion was the backdrop for Adlai E. Stevenson's unsuccessful presidential bid in 1952. When Stevenson was defeated, he composed his concession speech in his Mansion office. More recently, meetings were held in the Mansion with Cuban diplomats that resulted in Governor George Ryan's dramatic trips to Cuba.

The Mansion has a collection of priceless artwork, and each year 40,000 visitors come to see its treasures and hear its storied history. They see beautiful paintings by Francisco Goya and George Romney; the long, ancient table in the state dining room, around which our most renowned presidents and politicians have gathered; and the intricately carved furniture of Carthage farmer William J. Bartels. These great works of art came to the Mansion through the dedication of the Illinois Executive Mansion Association. A nonprofit corporation, the IEMA raised the funds to produce this book.

The Illinois Executive Mansion has been our home since 1999, but it belongs to the people of Illinois. Governor George H. Ryan and I would like to cordially invite one and all to visit our historic governor's residence, to hear its tales, and see its treasures.

Lura Lynn Ryan

Lura Lynn Ryan

WATERCOLOR ILLUSTRATIONS

	Page		Page
Lura Lynn and artist	*iii*	Children's tire swing	76
The Lincoln bedroom	12-13	Teddy bear	78
Garden Lamp	17	Mansion in spring	82
Lamps in the Lincoln bedroom	21	Overview of the east gardens.	86-87
Limoges vase	22	Entrance gate	91
Sweet Gum shade tree	23	Christmas	93
Steven A. Douglas chair	24	Garden entry	97
The fountain in the summer	26-27	The pole screen	98
The Yates bedroom	30	Closeup of Egyptian lions	99
Victorian mirrors	32	Music room piano	101
Yates' Bow front bureau	33	Egyptian lions	106-107
Lilies in the garden	35	Bartels fireplace	117
Meissen platter	36	East garden entrance	123
Porcelain lamp	37	North garden circular fountain	126-127
Fountain	38	Wrought iron stairway	134
The State Dining Room	40-41	Fireplace in the library	138
Window of the Mansion	46	The Illinois quilt	139
Jade vase and goblets	55	Bartels hand carved sofa	140
Pitcher, bowl, and soap dish	58	East garden trellis	141
Cherubs in the garden	61	West side of Mansion	144-145
Garden, looking down from the east porch	64-65	Living room private quarters	160
Fireplace in the library	71	East side of the mansion	162-163
Doll and paper cutouts	74	Breakfast area	174

The author wishes to acknowledge
the generous assistance he received while writing this book.

My heartfelt gratitude to

Maynard Crossland and Evelyn Taylor, Illinois Historic Preservation Agency,

Nita Crews and David Bourland, Illinois Executive Mansion,

Cheryl Schnirring,
Connie Butts,
Mary Michals,
Jim Helm,
Cheryl Pence,
Jennifer Ericson,
Jan Perone,

and the staff of the Illinois State Historical Library,

John Hoffmann, James Cornelius, and Robert Owens
of the indispensable Illinois Historical Survey,
University Library, University of Illinois at Urbana-Champaign

Lorin I. Nevling

Hill Chamerlik,
Chamerlik Design Ltd – Des Plaines, Illinois
for layout, design, and production

Illinois Governors
who have lived in the Executive Mansion

Joel A. Matteson	*1853-1857*
William H. Bissell	*1857-1860*
John Wood	*1860-1861*
Richard Yates	*1861-1865*
Richard J. Oglesby	*1865-1869 • Jan. 13-23, 1873 • 1885-1889*
John M. Palmer	*1869-1873*
John L. Beveridge	*1873-1877*
Shelby M. Cullom	*1877-1881 • 1881-1883*
John M. Hamilton	*1883-1885*
Joseph W. Fifer	*1889-1893*
John P. Altgeld	*1893-1897*
John R. Tanner	*1897-1901*
Richard Yates	*1901-1905*
Charles S. Deneen	*1905-1909 • 1909-1913*
Edward F. Dunne	*1913-1917*
Frank O. Lowden	*1917-1921*
Lennington Small	*1921-1925 • 1925-1929*
Louis L. Emmerson	*1929-1933*
Henry Horner	*1933-1937 • 1937-1940*
John H. Stelle	*1940-1941*
Dwight H. Green	*1941-1945 • 1945-1949*
Adlai E. Stevenson	*1949-1953*
William G. Stratton	*1953-1957 • 1957-1961*
Otto Kerner	*1961-1965 • 1965-1968*
Samuel H. Shapiro	*1968-1969*
Richard B. Ogilvie	*1969-1973*
Daniel Walker	*1973-77*
James R. Thompson	*1977-1979 • 1979-1983 • 1983-1987 • 1987-1991*
Jim Edgar	*1991-1995 • 1995-1999*
George H. Ryan	*1999-2003*

Contents

Foreward   *vii*

Watercolor Illustrations   *viii*

Acknowledgements   *ix*

Illinois Governors who have lived in the Executive Mansion   *x*

Contents   *xi*

Chapter 1:
1852-1860: The Birth of the Illinois Executive Mansion   *12*

Chapter 2:
1860-1868: Governors at War   *26*

Chapter 3:
1869-1901: Republican Ascendancy   *40*

Chapter 4:
1901-1921: A New Century   *64*

Chapter 5:
1921-1949: "Normalcy," Depression, War   *86*

Chapter 6:
1949-1961: Stevenson & Stratton, *Patrician & Plebeian*   *106*

Chapter 7:
1961-1973: Preserving the Illinois Executive Mansion   *126*

Chapter 8:
1973-1999: A New Executive Mansion   *144*

Chapter 9:
The Executive Mansion at the Turn of a New Century   *162*

Chapter 1

The Lincoln bedroom.

The Matteson family in Europe. Scandal forced the former governor to travel abroad.
Photo courtesy of the Illinois State Historical Library.

1852-1860: The Birth of the Illinois Executive Mansion

The first inhabitant of the Illinois Executive Mansion was Joel A. Matteson, a Democrat and successful Joliet businessman, who was elected governor of Illinois in 1852. Born in Watertown, New York, in 1808, Matteson worked in a variety of occupations as a young man. He was a store clerk, a teacher, and a railroad foreman. He married Mary Fish in 1832, and the young couple decided to go west to make their fortune, moving to Illinois the following year. Matteson was an enterprising fellow, a born businessman. Prior to departing New York, he packed his wagon, laden with possessions, with shoes and boots that he sold or traded on the journey. Since good boots were scarce on the frontier, he arrived in Illinois with more money than he had when he left New York. He farmed briefly in Kendall County before moving to Joliet where he became quite prosperous, owning a woolen mill, a store, and the city's first bank.[1]

Elected to the state legislature in 1842, Matteson served as chairman of the Senate finance committee. His business and legislative experience made him an attractive candidate for governor. Illinois was booming economically, her rich soil producing abundant harvests that needed only the completion of new railroads to be carried to distant markets. Yet the state government still groaned under a mountain of debt from earlier, misguided loans. Matteson's business acumen seemed to fit him perfectly to superintend the debt-ridden state government.[2]

Mr. & Mrs. Joel Matteson.
*Photo courtesy of the
Illinois State Historical Library.*

Matteson, his wife Mary, and their seven children arrived in the state capital of Springfield and made a gloomy discovery. The governor's home, at the corner of Eighth and Capitol, was a cramped structure that once housed the offices of the Illinois Board of Public Works. With the front door practically opened to the sidewalk, there was no yard for the younger children to roam and play. The new governor found the quarters confining for the weekly receptions he wished to hold for members of the state legislature when it was in session. Given to flamboyant tastes, Matteson's desire for luxury had grown even as his personal wealth had increased. He was not pleased with state housing. The growing state of Illinois required a new home for its governor of appropriate dignity and style.

Perhaps at the governor's urging, the state legislature appointed a commission to study the problem. Governor Matteson, the state auditor, and state treasurer–the commission–adopted Matteson's view and recommended that the state build a new residence for the governor. A lot was purchased at the corner of Edwards and Jackson streets, and an initial $15,000 appropriated for construction. Additional appropriations brought the final cost of the Mansion to more than $50,000. The new Mansion was opened to the public with a glittering reception on January 10, 1856, to which the social and political elite of the day was invited. One thousand invitations were purportedly sent. The success of the affair was marred when the gas lighting system failed because frigid winter temperatures froze the pipes. Nevertheless, candles were hastily lighted and the festivities continued. Newspaper accounts provided glowing descriptions of the reception. The <u>Illinois State Register</u> wrote that hundreds of guests from throughout Illinois partook of a supper "on a most munificent scale," and "the gayest assemblage ever marshalled in our city" enjoyed dancing and promenading to pleasant music. The <u>Illinois State Journal</u> declared: "In all respects, the entertainment was complete, and got up in a style of great magnificence–Gov. Matteson and his excellent lady doing the honors of host and hostess, with their well known hospitality . . . the party passed off in a most delightful manner." The following evening, the Mattesons opened the Mansion for a children's reception. John Todd Stuart, a former law partner of Abraham Lincoln, remembered that the rooms were ablaze with light, the gas system was functioning properly, and as a band merrily played "the children danced or at least hopped about . . . It was a beautiful sight and I never passed a more pleasant evening."[3]

The new Mansion.

Photo courtesy of the Illinois State Historical Library.

The new Mansion was the handiwork of John M. Van Osdel, a crusty, self-taught architect who designed many of the most prominent buildings in Illinois, including the

Cook County Court House and the Chicago City Hall. Van Osdel's Executive Mansion was Georgian in style with, somewhat incongruously, a Greek interior. Thomas Dennis of Springfield supervised construction and designed the interior woodwork which may explain the contrast between interior and exterior. It was a two-story building made of red-pressed brick provided by the Springfield firm of Eli Traintor, who boasted that his product was superior to brick produced in Baltimore and Philadelphia. Ornamental iron railing framed wide stone steps that led up to an entryway complete with a portico. Once inside the front door, visitors were greeted by an expansive hall that led into an antechamber, around which were six rooms connected by sliding doors that could be opened to create, in effect, one large room. A magnificent elliptical grand stairway, a brilliant Van Osdel touch, provided passage between floors. The basement consisted of two fuel rooms, laundry, kitchen, office, breakfast room, sink room, pantry, hall, and wine cellar. The building was crowned with an observatory that was fifteen feet above the roof. A well in the yard gave refreshing water that was, according to one visitor, "as cold as if iced."[4]

Garden Lamp.

Matteson and his family were gracious hosts with a gift for entertaining. They greatly enjoyed the Mansion and Springfield society. The first lady, Mary Fish Matteson, was both a devoted mother and accomplished hostess. She counted herself a relative of the renowned Fish family of New York, who boasted a string of political luminaries. Mary's daughter Clara sketched a tender and candid portrait of her mother. She described Mary as a tall, beautiful woman who retained much of her youthful figure throughout her life, even radiating attractiveness after death. Mary Matteson was given to what Clara characterized as an "undemonstrative nature," that is, she was reluctant to openly express her feelings, yet Clara remembered that by deed, rather than word, she and her siblings knew that they had their mother's deep affection.[5]

Mary Fish Matteson.
Photo courtesy of the Illinois State Historical Library.

Only on one tragic occasion did Mary Fish Matteson's stoic mask slip. Mary doted on her son Frederick, a precocious and promising lad who had received the best education possible in antebellum America. He attended a New Haven, Connecticut, prep school, then studied at Yale before embarking on three years of study at Heidelberg, Germany. He returned to Yale just as the Civil War began and, caught up in the patriotic fever that seizes young men at such moments, he abruptly left Yale for Springfield and a commission in the Yates Sharpshooters. The thought of so beloved a son going off to the hazards of war after a prolonged absence overseas was profoundly upsetting to Mary, who doggedly resisted the idea. Frederick was adamant, and when the day came for his departure, Clara witnessed a chilling and tragic scene. She remembered: "After the good-byes were said and the house seemed painfully quiet I heard the strangest sound, hardly like anything that could be made by a human being and I traced the cry to mother's room. I dared not enter alone so went in search of some one and found my sister Lydia to accompany me. It was indeed Mother and she was in the throes of mortal agony. She had borne the separation from my brother so bravely for three years when he was abroad but when he left her to enter the army,

Frederick Matteson in Civil War uniform.

Photo courtesy of the Illinois State Historical Library.

Clara Matteson Doolittle.

Photo courtesy of the Illinois State Historical Library.

she felt that she would never see him again in this world and that thought was too much for her." Similar scenes were taking place across the United States, as mothers tearfully embraced their boys, perhaps lovingly straightening a hat or smoothing a crease, before they marched away to uncertain fortunes.[6]

In a heartfelt effort to protect Frederick, Mary sent him a shirt made of chain. Frederick responded with a fatalistic acceptance of future events. He wrote Clara: "Thank Mother for the thought that prompted her to send the shirt, but if the finger of God has pointed me out as one of the victims of this war no armor can protect me and if not, I do not need it, as I would rather die than be thought a coward." Frederick had led a sheltered life, and his noble but pampered physique could not cope with the rough hygiene of the army camp, where more men succumbed to disease than bullets. He contracted typhoid fever and refused to countenance sick leave because that was the path shirkers were using to escape the hazards of combat. He died in camp, alone in a canvas tent, his cot soaked wet from fever. His mother received the tragic news in London via telegraph, and afterwards the memory was so painful that she could not speak Frederick's name. If a visitor tried to offer words of sympathy and comfort on Frederick's death, Mary, unable to cope, would impassively stride from the room, leaving the well-intentioned individual alone and dumbfounded. Clara recalled: "I am surprised that she lived through those years but she never referred to her sufferings and only those who loved her knew what she was going through."[7]

Joel Matteson was a reasonably popular governor who endeared himself to the Springfield community. When he announced that he would make it his home when his term concluded, even Springfield's Republican newspaper, the Illinois State Journal, declared, "We are gratified to learn that our worthy Governor intends to make Springfield his permanent home, when his present official term expires. Gov. Matteson will make an enterprising and most useful citizen, and will be an important acquisition to Springfield." A visitor to Springfield in 1856 found the community much improved from a visit four years previous and singled out the Executive Mansion as a particular gem. "The Governor's house is a fine specimen of architecture, and reflects abundant credit upon those who constructed it, and upon the State whose dignity it represents. Seldom have we seen a dwelling and its surroundings so well arranged, even those portions of our country where abundant wealth and opportunities give free scope to the fancy. It is not often that taste and economy are so well blended. There is no useless display–no extravagant waste of means; and no man who is raised to the high dignity of Governor of this State, should be surrounded with less beauty and honor. It is an object of honor and praise to this State, and no true citizen can look upon it without pride." The new Mansion seemed to crown Matteson's tenure with glory. The <u>Illinois State Journal</u> concluded Matteson's administration was "eminently successful."[8]

Matteson purchased a lot near the Executive Mansion, and construction soon began on an immense house that would be the new home for the former governor and his large brood. John M. Van Osdell designed this home too, the extensive grounds of which included a gardener's cottage, a double barn, and a grape conservatory that produced excellent grapes. However, Matteson's magnificent mansion came to be the symbol of one man's vast corruption rather than the social monument he had envisioned. It was discovered that while he was governor, Matteson had embezzled over $200,000 from the state treasury. He had come into possession of Illinois and Michigan Canal scrip already redeemed by the state. Matteson took the scrip and turned it in again, causing the state to pay a debt twice. In the ensuing scandal, Matteson escaped prison, agreeing to reimburse the state for the missing amount.[9]

He was now a man forever tainted by scandal. Republicans used Matteson's fraud to tar other Democrats, such as Stephen A. Douglas, as partners in corruption. They dubbed Matteson's Springfield mansion "Scrip Villa" and taunted the former governor on every occasion. Matteson may have escaped jail, but he could not escape social opprobrium. He was forced to travel abroad in an effort to avoid the public spotlight.

Matteson's Springfield Mansion, dubbed "Scrip Villa" by Republicans.

Photo courtesy of the Illinois State Historical Library.

In 1873 his magnificent Springfield residence burned to the ground, and Matteson died soon afterwards, heartbroken, his reputation in tatters. His wife Mary survived him by twenty-one years, dying peacefully at her daughter Clara's home.[10]

Matteson's successor was William H. Bissell, another man marked by tragedy, the state's first Republican governor whose victory in 1856 heralded a thirty-six-year Republican reign in the Executive Mansion. Born in New York in 1811, Bissell was trained as a physician and practiced briefly in New York before moving west and settling in Illinois. He took up politics as a Democrat, winning a seat in the state legislature in 1840. Service in the state legislature and perhaps the meager remuneration for a frontier physician persuaded him to change professions. He studied law and gained admission to the Illinois bar, practicing in Belleville.

In 1846 war broke out between the United States and Mexico, and Bissell volunteered for military service. He was elected colonel of the Second Illinois Regiment, which traveled to Mexico and was attached to the command of General Zachary

Governor William H. Bissell.
Photo courtesy of the
Illinois State Historical Library.

Taylor. Bissell distinguished himself, as did his regiment, at the Battle of Buena Vista. His command was in the worst of the fighting through much of the battle, suffering considerable casualties, and winning the praise of General Taylor. In the same action, other men with promising political careers ahead of them were killed: Henry Clay Jr. of Kentucky, son of the famous Whig senator, and John J. Hardin of Illinois. Bissell came out unscathed, or so it seemed at the time, and returned to Illinois and a hero's welcome.[11]

Elected to the U.S. House of Representatives in 1848, Bissell served three terms. He participated in the bitter sectional debate over the disposition of territory acquired in the Mexican War. Southern congressmen wished the territory opened to slavery, while many northern representatives wanted slavery confined to the states where it already existed. Bissell became a passionate advocate for restricting slavery. At a time when many congressmen carried loaded revolvers and heavy knives on the floor of Congress and when challenges to duel were not uncommon, Bissell was fearless. "The Southerners are insolent, overbearing & bullying beyond all endurance," he wrote from Washington in 1849. When a southern congressman questioned the valor of northern regiments at Buena Vista, and credited a Mississippi regiment commanded by Jefferson Davis, later the president of the Confederacy, with saving the day, Bissell was incensed. His rebuke drew a challenge to a duel from Jefferson Davis. The affair was adjusted without violence, but Illinois newspapers picked up the story and colorfully embellished it, declaring that Bissell had accepted the duel and had selected as his weapon an army musket loaded with ball and buckshot, a particularly lethal combination, the choice of which had prompted Jefferson Davis to withdraw his challenge. Thus, to Bissell's shining reputation as a soldier was added the myth that he had faced down an arrogant southern congressman, at a time when many in the North were heartily sick of southern bombast.[12]

Bissell's time in Congress estranged him from the Democratic party, which he concluded was too dominated by its southern wing, and he developed a strong admiration for Abraham Lincoln's political hero, Henry Clay. The Kansas-Nebraska Act, which permitted slavery in the Kansas and Nebraska territories if local citizens so desired, completed Bissell's alienation from the Democrats. In 1854 poor health forced his retirement from Congress. Two years later, the new Republican party was searching for a champion who could win a statewide election in overwhelmingly Democratic Illinois. As an antislavery Democrat with a fine war record, Bissell would attract Democrats to the Republican banner. Concerned at what he described as an effort to put Illinois in the command of the slave states, Bissell prepared to resume his political career despite faltering health.[13]

Lamps in the Lincoln bedroom. Etched glass and crystal.

Bissell's health was in steady decline throughout the 1850s. He traveled to spas and even to Cuba desperately seeking a cure, and while he experienced occasional mild improvement, his ailments became progressively worse. To compound the tragedy, the onset of disease roughly coincided with Bissell's marriage to the beautiful Elisabeth Kintzing Kane, daughter of Elias Kent Kane, former United States senator. Traveling to Washington, D.C., with her congressman husband, newlywed Elisabeth sent letters to her sister filled not with happy and giddy chatter, but with melancholy reports on the continued sickness of not only Colonel Bissell but also herself. In May 1854 Bissell became seriously ill, suffering paralysis in his legs that forced him to rely on crutches for the rest of his life.[14]

What was the cause of Bissell's malady? Bissell claimed that the paralysis was the result of a spinal injury he had suffered as a child. It was also attributed to chronic diarrhea that had afflicted him in Mexico. Others have concluded that his illness was most likely secondary syphilis contracted during his military service in Mexico. Some evidence exists to support the latter conclusion. Bissell's first wife, Emily Susan James, with whom he had had two daughters, died in 1844. Bissell seems to have become a merry widower who appreciated feminine beauty. As a new congressman in Washington, D.C., in 1849, he wrote: "I think I shall be well pleased with my situation here–though the presence of so many of the 'Divine Sex' as are congregated here is well calculated to keep a timid man like myself in a constant state of alarm and trepidation!" After Elisabeth's marriage to Bissell, her health, always precarious, seems to have declined. Letters from her sister Maria offer solace on persistent illnesses, which might mean that Bissell had infected his wife with the disease. Lincoln's close friend David Davis lamented Bissell's lack of "moral worth & stability of character." Whatever the cause, Bissell's illness altered and shortened his life.[15]

Selected by the Republican party as its candidate for governor in 1856, Bissell's health prevented him from embarking on the typically arduous campaign schedule. Nevertheless, the anti-Nebraska tide, that is, the prevailing sentiment against the expansion of slavery, swept him into the Executive Mansion. Democrats immediately suggested that Bissell would commit perjury if he took the oath of office because he had engaged in a duel with Jefferson Davis. The Illinois Constitution of 1848 required that state officers swear that they had never been participants in a duel. Republicans argued that the constitution's strictures applied only to duels within Illinois, and Bissell's affair of honor had occurred in the District of Columbia and was therefore exempt. While Jefferson Davis did issue a challenge and Bissell accepted, the affair had gone no further.[16]

On January 12, 1857, inauguration ceremonies took place in Springfield. Bissell's health remained uncertain. The paralysis of his legs hindered his mobility, leaving him an invalid. As a result, the swearing-in ceremony was held at the Executive Mansion, a harbinger of Bissell's work habits as governor. Poor health prompted Bissell to make the Mansion both his home and his office. At 2 p.m., Illinois legislators, state officials, judges, prominent citizens, and civic delegations gathered, and with outgoing Governor Matteson leading the way, marched in procession to the Executive Mansion. Once there, the crowd was crammed into the Mansion and watched as Justice John D. Caton of the Illinois Supreme Court administered the solemn oath of office to Bissell, who recited it without flinching at the anti-dueling avowal. The oath ceremony concluded, and the new governor greeted the assembled luminaries, perhaps seated in a chair or propped up on crutches.[17]

Limoges vase that was once owned by John Todd Stuart, Abraham Lincoln's first law partner, 1836.

Elisabeth Bissell found the social duties required of her at the Mansion, the unceasing social calls, receptions, and dinners, extremely fatiguing. Like her husband, Elisabeth's health was quite delicate, and she was prone to disabling "neuralgic attacks." Her stepdaughters, Josephine and Rhoda Bissell, were too young to be of much help. Elisabeth asked Gustave Koerner if his daughters Mary and Augusta would come to Springfield and assist her. Mary, then nineteen years old, agreed and found the routine busy indeed. Koerner remembered: "Almost every evening there was company at the house, card-playing, dancing, and musical entertainment." Koerner was pleased that his daughter was introduced to as fine a society as then existed in Illinois.[18]

Democrats savagely attacked Bissell, whom they regarded as a traitor for abandoning their party and joining the new Republican party. Immediately after Bissell's inauguration, Democrats accused him of violating the oath he had just taken, with

Sweet Gum shade trees grace the west approach to the Mansion.

its prohibition against dueling. They questioned his health and mental competence, charging him with having an "elastic conscience." It was suggested that Bissell's illness rendered him the weak and pliant tool of unscrupulous characters bent on manipulating the ailing governor for their own corrupt purposes. Bissell endured a vicious partisan assault throughout his tenure as governor. His biographer argued that Bissell was deeply hurt by the hateful rhetoric his opponents directed at him, an ordeal that further damaged his shattered physical constitution.[19]

There is considerable evidence that, with health impaired and spirits sometimes flagging under the rhetorical barrage, Bissell relied on Abraham Lincoln. He consulted Lincoln on the preparation of his inaugural address, specifically requesting that Lincoln write a statement on the ongoing slavery extension controversy. Bissell mistakenly signed a Democratic apportionment bill late in the legislative session in 1857, then upon recognizing his mistake, erased his signature. Democrats claimed that once a bill had been signed, it was law. The case went before the Illinois Supreme Court with Lincoln and another attorney representing Bissell. The court ruled that Bissell could withdraw his approval. When Bissell vetoed another Democratic apportionment bill two years later, Lincoln wrote the accompanying veto message. Ebenezer Lane, who ran the Illinois Central Railroad, called Lincoln "the acknowledged special advisor of the Bissell administration." Bissell allowed Lincoln to work in the vacant governor's office in the State Capitol building on the city's square.[20]

Bissell's health deteriorated precipitously early in 1860. On March 13, 1860, a local newspaper reported that the governor had a "violent cold," which rapidly progressed to pneumonia and fever. Physicians were summoned to the Mansion and ministered to the failing governor, including one doctor who came by train from St. Louis. But in those days before antibiotics, they could do little. On March 14, Abraham Lincoln returned to Springfield from a successful trip to the East, a journey highlighted by his famed address at the Cooper Union in New York City, a speech that closed with the stirring admonition: "Let us have faith that right makes might, and in that faith, let us, to the end, dare to do our duty as we understand it." Bissell had done his duty in peace and in war, and in the fight against slavery's expansion, but he was not fated to continue the struggle with his friend Lincoln in the great conflict looming on the horizon. Three days after Lincoln stepped down from the train, Bissell felt the approach of death and summoned his family and servants to his bedside in the Mansion, taking leave of each with tender remarks. Soon after, Bissell's political confidants arrived for a final visit. Abraham Lincoln, his law partner William H. Herndon, Ozias M. Hatch, and Jesse K. Dubois, leading Republicans all, their faces masks of sorrow, climbed the Mansion's spiral stairway to comfort and bid farewell to their friend and political colleague as his reckoning approached. The next day, March 18, Bissell uttered a last prayer, then lapsed into a peaceful silence and died.[21]

One of a set of hand-carved custom chairs made for Steven A. Douglas. The legs are purposely short to accommodate his small stature.

Services for Governor Bissell were held on March 21, 1860. The Executive Mansion, Springfield's public buildings, and many businesses were draped in mourning. Bissell had converted to Catholicism, and accordingly, Catholic funeral rites were performed. His remains were placed in a simple coffin and lay in state in the west parlor of the Mansion, a crucifix and candles at the head of the coffin. Bissell was dressed in a black suit, and his face bore a "placid and natural" expression. Civic and military delegations formed up and marched to the Mansion, where shortly after 10 a.m., the procession escorted Bissell's remains to the cemetery. Militia units were drawn up in square around Bissell's grave, as Mexican War veterans acting as pall bearers conducted the governor to his final rest. A crowd estimated at five thousand to eight thousand had gathered to witness the solemn ritual. After gravesite rites, the militia assembled in column and noisily departed, their rifles banging on cartridge belts, boots thumping on the soft spring earth, trampling the green shoots of grass emerging from winter's grip. The crowd gradually departed, many casting back looks of sorrow and grief as they walked away. The Chicago Tribune pronounced a fitting epitaph for Bissell: "When others would have succumbed to physical pain and the wasting process of disease, with the heroism of a lofty nature, with a most indomitable will, and with a courage that never quailed, he continued to give his mind to public duties to the last, and finally yielded up his life with all his armor on."[22]

Endnotes

1 James T. Hickey, ed., "An Illinois First Family: The Reminiscences of Clara Matteson Doolittle," Journal of the Illinois State Historical Society, 69 (Feb. 1976), 3-7. The History of Will County (Chicago: Wm. Le Baron, Jr. and Co., 1978), 317-19, 407.

2 Octavia Roberts Corneau, "The Governor's Mansion, 1853-1953: A Social History of the Illinois Executive Mansion," 4-5, Octavia Roberts Corneau Collection, IHSL.

3 Illinois State Journal, Jan. 11, 1856, pg. 3, c. 1, Mar. 11, 1856, pg. 3, c. 1. Illinois State Register, Jan. 11, 1856, pg. 3, c. 1. John T. Stuart to Bettie, Jan. 13, 1856, Stuart-Hay Collection, ISHL. Corneau, 6.

4 "John M. Van Osdel," Biographical Sketches of the Leading Men of Chicago (Chicago: Wilson and St. Clair, 1868), 91-95. "John M. Van Osdel: Pioneer Architect of Chicago," Cook-Witter Report (July 12, 2000). Alton Daily Courier, Aug. 4, 1854 and St. Louis Intelligencer in Illinois State Journal, Aug. 25, 1854, both in "The Governor's Mansion a Century Ago," Journal of the Illinois State Historical Society, vol. 48 (Autumn 1955), 330-37.

5 James. T. Hickey, ed., "An Illinois First Family: The Reminiscences of Clara Matteson Doolittle," Journal of the Illinois State Historical Society, 69 (Feb. 1976), 3-16.

6 Hickey, ed., "Clara Diary," 12.

7 Ibid., 11-13.

8 Illinois State Journal, Mar. 11, 1856, pg. 3, c. 1 and Jan. 7, 1857, pg. 2, c. 1-2. Chicago Times, Dec. 6, 1856 in Illinois State Journal, Dec. 15, 1856, pg. 2, c. 3.

9 Hickey, ed., "Clara Diary," 11. Robert P. Howard, "The Great Canal Scrip Fraud: The Downfall of Governor Joel A. Matteson," 1980 Selected Papers in Illinois History (Springfield, 1982).

10 Illinois State Journal, July 31, 1860, pg. 2, c. 4. Hickey, ed., "Clara Diary," 14.

11 Jack Trout, "William H. Bissell: Anti-Nebraska Democrat and First Republican Governor of Illinois," (M.A. Thesis, Illinois State University, 1962), 54-61.

12 Bissell to Joseph Gillispie, House of Reps, Wash. D.C., Feb. 12, [1850], Gillespie Collection, ISHL. Donald F. Tingley, "The Jefferson Davis-William H. Bissell Duel," Mid-America, 38 (1956), 146-55.

13 Bissell to Joseph Gillispie, House of Reps, Wash. D.C., Feb. 12, [1850], Bissell to Gillispie, Wash., Apr. 19, 1850, Bissell to E. Peck, Belleville, Jan. 21, 1856, Joseph Gillespie Collection, ISHL.

14 Maria to Lizzie, Dec. 21, 1851, Jan. 18, 1852, Feb. 1, Mar. 12, June 22, 1853, Kane-Bissell Collection, ISHL. Illinois State Journal, Mar. 19, 1860, pg. 2, c. 1. Trout, 112-13.

15 Trout, 112-13. Illinois State Journal, Mar. 19, 1860, pg. 2, c. 1. Bissell to Joseph Gillespie, Wash. D.C., Dec. 15, 1849, Joseph Gillespie Collection, ISHL. Maria to Liz, Belleville, Ills., Jan. 10, 1852, Jan. 18, 1852, Feb. 15, 1852, Kane-Bissell Collection, ISHL. David Davis to William P. Walker, June 25, 1847, David Davis Collection, ISHL.

16 Tingley, 146-55. Illinois State Journal, Aug. 9, 1856, pg. 2, c. 4.

17 Illinois State Journal, Jan. 13, 1857, pg. 2, c. 2.

18 Thomas J. McCormack, ed., Memoirs of Gustave Koerner, 1809-1896, vol. 2 (Cedar Rapids: The Torch Press, 1909), 40.

19 Trout, 171-73, 186-87, 198-202.

20 Bissell to Lincoln, Jan. 2, 1857, Robert Todd Lincoln Collection, quoted in Trout, 171. McCormack, ed., Memoirs of Koerner, vol. 2, 38. Trout, 174, 198-203. Charles Leroy Brown, "Abraham Lincoln and the Illinois Central Railroad, 1857-1860," Journal of the Illinois State Historical Society, 36 (July 1943), 150-51. John J. Duff, A. Lincoln, Prairie Lawyer (New York: Rinehart & Co., Inc., 1960), 246.

21 Illinois State Journal, Mar. 13, 1860, pg. 2, c. 1, Mar. 15, 1860, pg. 2, c. 1, Mar. 19, 1860, pg. 2, c. 1. Trout, 212-13.

22 Illinois State Register, Mar. 20, 1860, pg. 3, c. 2, Mar. 22, 1860, pg. 2, c. 1, Mar. 27, 1860, pg. 2, c. 2. Chicago Press and Tribune in Illinois State Journal, Mar. 21, 1860, pg. 2, c. 1-2, Mar. 22, 1860, pg. 2, c. 2.

Chapter 2

The fountain in the summer of 1999.

Due to a severe drought, water could not be used. The fountain was filled with cascading "Brugmansia" commonly called "angel trumpets".

Fay Smith

Governor Richard Yates defiantly glares into the camera. He was a man of passionate intensity.

Photo courtesy of the Illinois State Historical Library.

1860-1868: Governors at War

With Governor Bissell's death, Lieutenant Governor John Wood assumed the duties of governor of Illinois. A modest and decent man, Wood allowed the Bissell family to remain in the Mansion for the final months of their late patriarch's term. In the tumultuous election of 1860, which brought Abraham Lincoln to the White House and the nation to the brink of civil war, Republican Richard Yates was elected governor. Like Lincoln, Yates was a transplanted Kentuckian whose family migrated to Sangamon County in 1831. Yates graduated from Illinois College, studied law, and began his career as a lawyer in Jacksonville. He and his wife Catharine had five children.[1]

Yates did not possess Lincoln's intellectual gifts or steely self-possession. He was a passionate, high-strung man who lashed out at those who annoyed him. When an Indiana resident wrote to criticize Yates's appointment of Orville Hickman Browning to the U.S. Senate in place of Stephen A. Douglas, who had died, Yates responded: "I should not reply to your insulting letter except to say to you to mind your own business . . . all I have to say is that you are guilty of meanness and falsehood–and I would thank you, not to trouble me with your silly advice." This is the type of insulting letter that Lincoln might write for the emotional catharsis but never mail, filing it away in his desk. Yet Yates's passionate nature was the key to his political success, as he was a talented, emotionally charged speaker capable of whipping up a crowd. Once he became governor, Yates practiced his speeches late into the evening before a mirror in a Mansion drawing room, perfecting his gestures and the inflection of his voice.[2]

Yates would need all of his oratorical skills during his tenure as governor, for within a few months of his inaugural, the country descended into civil war. A devoted Unionist, Yates plunged wholeheartedly into the task of raising and outfitting Illinois troops. He made countless recruiting speeches, exhorting young men to rally to the colors to defend the Union and the Constitution at their most perilous hour. At this he was most successful, as thousands of Illinoisans volunteered for the Union army, and their regiments won glory in some of worst fighting of the war.[3]

Equipping and training tens of thousands of troops was daunting indeed. Yates grappled with countless problems, assisted by a staff that was miniscule by twentieth-century standards. He was plagued by office-seekers, bombarded by callers at the Mansion, so many that he was forced to restrict the hours he devoted to receiving visitors. His incoming correspondence was staggering in its size and scope. His office was flooded with letters requesting appointments in the new regiments being organized and in state government. Supplicants petitioned the harried governor for positions such as wagon master, surgeon, chaplain, paymaster, purchasing agent, staff officer, drill master, and fifer. One central Illinois physician even requested

appointment as the the official "embalmer" of the Illinois war dead. Many letters warned of impending doom for Cairo in southern Illinois, suggesting that a Confederate invasion was imminent. Yates, with the help of his secretary John Moses, had to sift through and respond to these countless queries.[4]

Suddenly the headquarters of a massive military recruiting effort, Springfield resembled an armed camp. Soldiers training at nearby Camp Butler came into the city in search of whiskey and trouble. They often found it, brawling with other soldiers and citizens; the Springfield police reported 1,514 arrests in 1861. "There are altogether too many shoulder straps at the hotels, saloons, and billiard rooms of the city," lamented the Illinois State Journal. Regiments heading south passed through town, including famed orator Robert G. Ingersoll's cavalry unit, which formed a column a mile in length as it negotiated Springfield's streets. After the first Union victories, thousands of Confederate prisoners arrived for imprisonment at Camp Butler, giving local citizens a glimpse of the enemy, whom they found rather unprepossessing.[5]

Still, in the midst of war, the social amenities of civilization were preserved, as when Governor Yates held a glittering reception for the members of a convention meeting in Springfield to draft a new state constitution. On January 29, 1862, guests called at the Executive Mansion between 8 and 9

Catharine Geers Yates witnessed inaugural ceremonies for her husband and son as Illinois governor. Some believe her spirit haunts the Mansion.

Photo Courtesy of the Illinois State Historical Library.

The Yates bedroom.

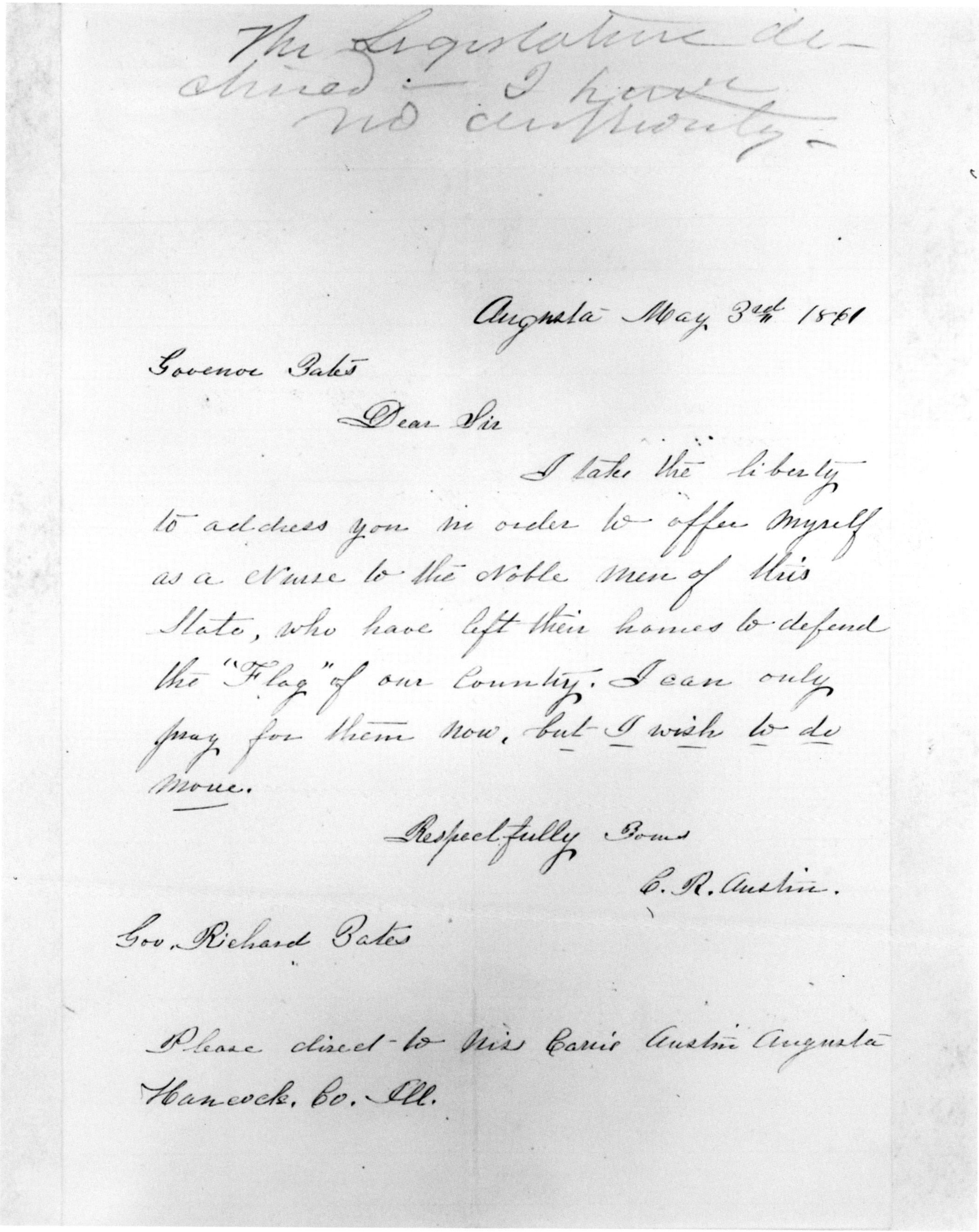

*The Legislature de-
sired — I have
no authority —*

Augusta May 3rd 1861

Governor Yates

    Dear Sir

        I take the liberty
to address you in order to offer myself
as a Nurse to the Noble men of this
State, who have left their homes to defend
the "Flag" of our Country. I can only
pray for them now, but I wish to do
more.

        Respectfully Yours

            C. R. Austin.

Gov. Richard Yates

Please direct to Mrs Carrie Austin Augusta
Hancock. Co. Ill.

Women too found the times stirring and wished to do their part. In this letter of May 3, 1861, Carrie Austin asked Governor Yates for an appointment as a nurse. *Photo courtesy of the Illinois State Historical Library.*

David Smith of Peoria, Illinois, who served in the 47th Illinois Infantry. Smith died on September 30, 1864. Yates was haunted by the knowledge that he was sending young men like Smith to certain death.

Photo courtesy of the Illinois State Historical Library.

The elegant Victorian mirrors in the state dining room, shown festooned for Christmas, belonged to Governor Yates. He let them remain in the Mansion when he left office.

p.m. Governor Yates cordially greeted each guest in the northeast parlor, introducing his wife Catharine and other relatives. The Mansion had recently been redecorated, and the result earned appreciative remarks. "Rich Wilton carpets, velvet, of the medallion pattern" elegantly covered the floor, while silk damask curtains draped the windows. Full-length mirrors of French glass accentuated the beauty of the furnishings. Drawing rooms were tastefully furnished with chairs and sofas of rosewood and brocatelle and with rosewood tables that had polished marble surfaces. The staff served a sumptuous repast in the east suite of rooms. Guests found a table in the shape of a double cross crowded with boned turkeys and sugar-cured hams, oysters, fruits, and tempting desserts "frosted and adorned with all the cunning of the confectioner's art." The evening was judged a great success; Governor Yates and his family were most delightful hosts.[6]

That pleasant occasion was an exception amid the ponderous labors of a governor in wartime. Illinois regiments often suffered staggering casualties, sometimes more than fifty percent in some regiments were killed or wounded. Yates made it his personal mission to do everything possible for the young Illinois men who had marched fearlessly off to war. Yates's son speculated that his father felt a great sense of responsibility for the welfare of the men because he had helped to recruit them. His tireless efforts on their behalf earned him the welcome nickname "The Soldiers' Friend."[10]

The governor's devotion to the troops caused him considerable political grief. Yates had called the state legislature into special session immediately after the war's inception. Requesting war measures, he informed the legislators in bloodcurdling tones, "Our people will wade through seas of blood before they will see a single star or a solitary stripe erased from the glorious flag of our Union." An appropriation was duly passed to clothe and equip Illinois troops. Unfortunately the funds were soon exhausted, and Yates was forced to continue to spend state funds without legislative authorization. He could do little else. The federal government planned to assume the responsibility of supplying Illinois troops, but the transfer was delayed. Democrats accused Yates of violating his authority, bungling his duties, and even outright corruption. "Gov. Yates has never been suspected of possessing a dangerous amount of brains," intoned the Democratic Chicago Times. Yates considered Democratic actions treasonous, and his contentious relationship with Illinois Democrats led him to take the extraordinary step of proroguing the state legislature in 1863. Yates could be quite difficult–he quarreled with President Lincoln over the distribution of patronage, and he even publicly attacked Lincoln for not prosecuting the war with sufficient vigor[8]

Yates's operations may indeed have skirted conventional legal and budgetary channels, but it was after all war, and his genuine affection and concern for the ordinary soldier was certainly meritorious. After the Union victories at Fort Henry, Fort Donelson, and Shiloh, the latter particularly costly in casualties, Yates personally traveled to the still-smoldering battlefields and arranged for the delivery of additional surgeons, nurses, and medical supplies. He ordered the steamboat that had carried him to the Shiloh battlefield to be filled with Illinois wounded, who were then transported to hospitals. He appointed agents to scour the battlefields and hospitals, recording the names of the dead and wounded so that Illinois families could receive the most accurate accounting of the fate of their sons, fathers, and husbands in uniform. "It is sincerely to be hoped that not a single name of these gallant men whose prowess has reflected such imperishable lustre upon the State and the country shall remain unrecorded," Yates wrote in a report on the Fort Donelson casualties.[9]

Governor Richard J. Oglesby in the uniform of a Civil War general.

Photo courtesy of the Illinois State Historical Library.

Yates's service as governor was rewarded with his elevation to the United States Senate in 1864. However, his years of arduous service in wartime state government and the long separations from his family necessitated by service in the Senate exacerbated a personal problem. Yates had struggled throughout his life with an addiction to alcohol. He had taken the temperance pledge on a number of occasions and had even spoken at temperance meetings, only to succumb to temptation, each instance of failure a blow to his morale and personal esteem. When poor health forced Catharine to remain in Illinois, leaving him alone in Washington, Yates wrote his wife plaintive letters of apology for his bad behavior during binges: "My dearest wife you have been very kind and good to me and under the influence of liquor I have treated you with an unkindness for which I can only ask your forgiveness." And again: "Won't you forget and forgive and love me still? Whatever may have happened my love for you has never failed or lessened . . . and never would I have done wrong but for liquor." During the impeachment trial of Andrew Johnson, Yates was absent from the Senate a great deal, angering Illinois Republicans who wanted their senator present at that most crucial moment. Republican newspapers called for his resignation, and Yates was forced to write a humiliating public confession in which he pledged yet again to abstain from liquor. Tragically, his alcoholism became progressively worse, ending his political career and compromising his health. He died of a heart attack in St. Louis on November 27, 1873. He lies in a quiet cemetery in Jacksonville, united in death with the young soldiers who loved him as "The Soldiers' Friend."[10]

Yates' Bow front bureau.

Yates's successor was Richard J. Oglesby, another Republican and the first of a number of Civil War veterans to occupy the Executive Mansion. Amazingly, this was the first of what would prove to be three nonconsecutive terms as governor for Ogelsby.

Members of Company E, 47th Regiment, Illinois Infantry at Oxford, Mississippi, December 18, 1862. They were the young men whom Yates recruited and Oglesby led in the Civil War.

Photo courtesy of the Illinois State Historical Library.

Before he became governor, Oglesby had led a rich life of great adventures and challenges. Born in Oldham County, Kentucky, in 1824, Oglesby was orphaned at the age of eight when both parents and three siblings died in a cholera epidemic. He was taken to the home of an uncle, who later moved to Decatur, Illinois, in 1836, much as Abraham Lincoln's family had in 1830. The family scratched out a living from the soil. Richard received the typically rudimentary education of a frontier youth. He demonstrated some talent for public speaking, at the age of eighteen delivering the Fourth of July speech in Decatur, and he gravitated to the law as a profession. After a brief apprenticeship in another lawyer's office, the customary route to practice in those days, Oglesby was admitted to the bar in 1845 and began his professional career in Sullivan and Decatur.[11]

Young Oglesby was soon swept up in the war fever that gripped Illinois with the declaration of war against Mexico in May 1846. He served as a lieutenant in the Fourth Illinois Regiment. Among his wartime exploits: he helped put down a riot of American troops, and it was falsely reported in hometown newspapers that he had been fatally wounded during the incident; he and his regiment marched 450 miles across Mexico to join the forces of General Winfield Scott, poised for the campaign on Mexico City; and he saw action in the ensuing battles of Vera Cruz and Cerro Gordo. Oglesby returned home a veteran of America's first foreign war.[12]

He embarked on another adventure when gold was discovered in California in 1849, joining the mass exodus of young fortune-seekers flocking to the gold fields. They traveled across what was then a vast wilderness, driving six-mule teams that hauled wagons of provisions. Oglesby's foray into the gold fields was a success. He came home to Decatur in 1851 with $5,000 in gold that he invested in area real estate. His windfall led to another adventure, a trip to Europe and the Middle East, quite a perilous undertaking in the days before reliable travel and medical care. Something of a skeptic concerning religion, Oglesby's tour of the fabled sites of Christianity did not convert him into a believer. He later became a great friend of the renowned agnostic Robert G. Ingersoll of Peoria. Back in Illinois, Oglesby began to give lectures on the Holy Land. These popular talks proved a path into politics–Oglesby ran for Congress as a Republican in 1858. Losing his bid, Oglesby remained active in Republican politics and was elected to the state legislature in 1860. He also coined Lincoln's popular campaign nickname, the "rail-splitter," reminding the electorate of the common-man origins of the prosperous Springfield attorney.[13]

When the Civil War began, the adventuresome Oglesby resigned from the state senate and organized his own regiment, the Eighth Illinois Infantry. Colonel Oglesby was soon marching south to protect Cairo from rumored Confederate assault. He later came under the command of the then obscure, scruffy Ulysses S. Grant. Oglesby was quickly promoted to brigadier-general after successfully leading a brigade at the battle of Fort Donelson. He was severely wounded near Corinth, Mississippi, and he carried the ball in his chest for the remainder of his life. Plagued by the effects of his wound, Oglesby resigned his commission to run for governor in 1864.[14]

Lilies in the Garden.

Lawyer, gold prospector, world traveler and lecturer, congressional candidate, state legislator, and twice a soldier, Oglesby arrived at the Executive Mansion having had many interesting, and in some ways fortunate, experiences. He was an affable man, "geniality and thorough good nature are predominant traits," said a contemporary, and he had a pronounced sense of humor. Biographer Mark Plummer noted that Oglesby possessed the rare ability to retain the friendship of political foes. But the ball that nearly killed him at Corinth seems in retrospect an ill-tiding of future calamities. Often it seems that those who achieve great success are fated to bear an equal measure of sorrow. The deaths of Willie Lincoln in the first year of his father's presidency and of young Benjamin Pierce just before his father Franklin was sworn in as president spring to mind, as their successful parents were laid low in mourning. Oglesby and his wife Anna were to endure a similar tragedy. One week before he was to be inaugurated as governor, Oglesby's young son Richard, who was affectionately known as "Dickie," died of diphtheria on January 9, 1865. He was six years old. Devastated, Oglesby requested a one-week postponement of the inauguration ceremonies. Governor Yates was agreeable, so the official swearing in occurred on January 16, 1865.[15]

Meissen platter, white with purple violets, belonged to Mary Todd Lincoln. A gift from Robert Todd Lincoln Beckwith.

To his immense credit, Oglesby proposed in his inaugural address the repeal of Illinois' repulsive Black Laws, which placed onerous restrictions on African-American citizens. He also strongly endorsed the Thirteenth Amendment, which abolished slavery in the United States. The Republican-dominated General Assembly promptly ended the infamous Black Laws and became the first state legislature to ratify the Thirteenth Amendment. In his famous 1858 debates with Stephen A. Douglas, Abraham Lincoln had insisted that a black man had the same "right to eat the bread without leave of anybody else which his own hand earns." Richard Oglesby and the Republican General Assembly took a tentative step on the path to racial justice in Illinois, fulfilling Lincoln's political legacy.[16]

The dark cloud of death followed Governor Oglesby when he traveled to Washington, D.C., in April 1865. Accompanied by Illinois Adjutant-General Isham Haynie, Oglesby arrived on April 14. He had a cordial reunion with Abraham Lincoln at the White House. The president was in fine humor. Robert E. Lee's Army of Northern Virginia had surrendered five days previously, and Lincoln amused himself and his Illinois friends by reading excerpts from humorist Petroleum V. Nasby. That evening Lincoln attended a play at Ford's Theatre. In the third act, John Wilkes Booth entered the presidential box and shot Lincoln in the back of the head. Oglesby and Haynie were awakened at their hotel and rushed to the home where the fatally wounded president had been taken. Sadly, nothing could be done, and Oglesby witnessed the death throes of his friend.[17]

After Lincoln's demise, Oglesby played a prominent role in arranging for the president's spectacular funeral. He helped persuade Mary Lincoln to inter the body in Springfield, and he accompanied the presidential remains on the fourteen-day journey home. On May 4, 1865, services were held in Springfield, and Lincoln's hearse passed the Executive Mansion on the way to his final resting place at Oak Ridge Cemetery. Governor Oglesby held a reception at the Mansion that evening for state mourning delegations who had attended the funeral. He became president of the Lincoln Monument Association, which strove to build a suitable tomb and monument for the martyred president.[18]

Not all was gloom during Oglesby's tenure as governor. On October 8, 1865, Anna gave birth to a son, whom the proud parents named Robert. His arrival helped to heal the trauma of little Dickie's death. The Oglesbys also enjoyed the social activities that came with residence in the Illinois Executive Mansion. The season typically coincided with sessions of the Illinois legislature. During the winter of 1867, Governor Oglesby and his wife held three parties or "levees" at the Mansion: January 22, February 7, and February 28, the last a masquerade ball![19]

The most elaborate surviving account exists of the party given on January 22. Guests began arriving at nine that evening, and, in an age before electricity, were amazed at the brilliancy of the brightly lit Mansion. Once inside, guests noticed that American flags decorated the doorframes and the balustrade of the Mansion's famed winding staircase. Flowers and other decorations were tastefully arranged about the rooms. Coats were deposited in the cloakroom, and then guests descended the stairs to greet Governor and Mrs. Oglesby, who cordially received their visitors in the southeast parlor. Oglesby's unpretentious manner lent an air of sociability, even informality, to the occasion. State officers, members of the General Assembly, judges, and citizens mingled together, an estimated five hundred in all.[20]

At 11 p.m. a late supper was served in a parlor located behind the reception area. Meanwhile, the basement had been reserved as a retreat for the men, and they trooped down the stairs to enjoy cold meats, crackers, wine, and cigars. Oglesby was fond of bourbon, so perhaps he shared an amber tumbler of that too. An orchestra at the foot of the stairs on the main floor began to play, and young and old danced, many continuing into the early hours. Oglesby's party was "one of the most pleasant and delightful occasions ever enjoyed in the State Capital."[21]

A similarly glittering reception occurred on February 7, and again lasted past midnight. The masquerade ball of February 28 was also judged a success, as the costumed guests "played their respective parts with a life-like truthfulness." The governor and his wife again offered a sumptuous repast, the orchestra provided entertainment, and the costumes included a king and peasant, a queen and flower girl, clergyman, monk with cowl, and southern planter.[22]

These moments of pleasure were hopefully savored by the Oglesbys because tragedy was to revisit them. That summer Anna Oglesby became ill with the awful symptoms of that incurable scourge of the nineteenth century, tuberculosis. In July

Porcelain lamp,
Paris, France – Circa 1860.

the governor took his ailing wife north to Minnesota in an effort to escape the oppressive heat and humidity of the Springfield summer. They returned to Illinois at the end of August, the newspapers reporting that Anna's health was much improved. Any improvement was temporary, and by October the situation was described as "critical." The governor remained close to his wife throughout her illness, refusing many invitations to speak and playing a less prominent political role than he would have under normal circumstances.[23]

The following spring Oglesby proclaimed April 15, the third anniversary of Lincoln's death, a day of fasting and prayer. Across the state, businesses closed for the day, and churches held services. In Springfield, services were conducted in the State House, with Governor Oglesby in attendance. Perhaps he put aside his religious skepticism that day and said a prayer for Anna.[24]

Anna Oglesby died in the Executive Mansion on June 4, 1868, her thin frame a testament to the ravages of tuberculosis. The Reverend A. B. Carpenter officiated at her funeral, which was held at the Mansion two days later. Oglesby had chartered a special train to convey Anna home to Decatur, where she was buried next to the two children who had preceded her in death. Reflecting on his young wife's death at age thirty-two, Oglesby wrote: "My dear Anna suffered long but suffers no more. She has left me with our sweet little children for a heavenly home. She died as only the happy can die." Haunted by the memory of his wife, Governor Oglesby spent the next five months away from Springfield.[25]

Although marred by tragedy, Oglesby's first term in the Executive Mansion was a substantive one. He carried through important civil rights protections for African-Americans and continued Yates's policy of caring for soldiers and their dependents. He shepherded the creation of the Illinois Industrial University (the future University of Illinois), a new capitol building for state government, and a penitentiary. He labored to raise money for a suitable monument for Abraham Lincoln. Tragedy did not prevent Richard J. Oglesby from serving the people of Illinois.

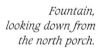

Fountain, looking down from the north porch.

Endnotes

1 Robert P. Howard, <u>Mostly Good and Competent Men</u> (1988; reprint, Springfield: University of Illinois at Springfield, 1999), 95, 102-104.

2 Richard Yates to M.C. Hunter, June 18, 1861, Yates Family Papers, ISHL. Richard Yates and Catherine Yates Pickering, <u>Richard Yates: Civil War Governor</u>, ed. John H. Krenkel (Danville, IL: Interstate Printers and Publishers, Inc., 1966), 168-69.

3 Jack Nortrup, "Richard Yates: A Personal Glimpse of the Illinois Soldiers' Friend," <u>Journal of the Illinois State Historical Society</u>, 56 (Summer 1963), 122-26.

4 Chas. W. Myer to Yates, Carlyle, Mar. 1, 1861, Sophie Wheeler to Yates, Elgin, Apr. 26, 1861, appointment as embalmer, Benjamin Woodward, M.D. to Yates, Galesburg, June 26, 1861, Yates Family Collection, ISHL.

5 <u>Illinois State Journal</u>, Jan. 16, 1862, pg. 3, c. 3, Jan. 30, 1862, pg 3, c. 3, Feb. 21, 1862, pg. 3, c. 4, Mar. 1, 1862, pg. 3, c. 2.

6 <u>Illinois State Journal</u>, Jan. 29, 1862, pg. 2, c. 1, Jan. 31, 1862, pg. 3, c. 5, Feb. 11, 1862, pg. 1, c. 2-3.

7 Krenkel, 187-93.

8 Mark A. Plummer, professor emeritus at Illinois State University, was kind enough to share a draft manuscript of his biography of Governor Oglesby. The notes below denoted Plummer et al are from that draft manuscript. Professor Plummer's important biography, <u>Lincoln's Rail-Splitter: Governor Richard J. Oglesby</u>, has been published by the University of Illinois Press. Mark A. Plummer, "Martial Spirit," 11-12. <u>Chicago Times</u>, Nov. 5, 1862 in Jack Nortrup, "Yates, the Prorogued Legislature, and the Constitutional Convention," <u>Journal of the Illinois State Historical Society</u>, 62 (Spring 1969), 21. Krenkel, 154, 156-59, 173-75.

9 <u>Illinois State Journal</u>, Jan. 29, 1862, pg. 2, c. 3, Feb. 27, 1862, pg. 2, c. 2, Apr. 19, 1862, pg. 2, c. 2, Apr. 24, 1862, pg. 2, c. 5-6, Ft Donelson report, Mar. 10, 1862, pg. 2, c. 2-5.

10 Jno. M. Snyder to Gov. Yates, Springfield, May 14, 1866, Krenkel, 249, Yates to Katy, Wash., D.C., Apr. 24, 1868, Krenkel, 272-73, Yates to Katie, Wash., D.C., May 31, 1868, Krenkel, 273-74. <u>Illinois State Journal</u>, Apr. 4, 1868, pg. 1, c. 2, Apr. 8, 1868, pg. 2, c. 3, Apr. 27, 1868, pg. 2, c. 3-4.

11 Plummer, "An Orphan Boy," 3-8.

12 Plummer, "An Orphan Boy," 8-15.

13 Plummer, "An Orphan Boy," 16-20, "A Young American Abroad," 6-26, "The Rail-Splitter," 1-14, 17-23.

14 Plummer, "Martial Spirit," 13-38, "An Intimate Personal Friend," 1-30.

15 Plummer, "An Orphan Boy," 3, "Martial Spirit," 8, "Governor, 1865-1869," 1-2. <u>Illinois State Journal</u>, Jan. 10, 1865, pg. 2, c.1, Jan. 11, 1865, pg. 2, c. 1, Jan. 17, 1865, pg. 2, c. 1.

16 Illinois State Journal, Jan. 17, 1865, pg. 2, c. 1. Plummer, "Governor, 1865-69," 1-3. Arthur Charles Cole, <u>The Era of the Civil War, 1848-1870</u> (1919; reprint, Urbana: University of Illinois Press, 1987), 225-29, 388.

17 Mark A. Plummer, "The Last Hours of Lincoln: The Haynie Diary," <u>Journal of Illinois History</u>, 4 (Spring 2001), 25-40.

18 Plummer, "The Lincoln Icon," 8-13.

19 Plummer, "Governor, 1865-69," 22. <u>Illinois State Journal</u>, Jan. 23, 1867, pg. 4, c. 4, Feb. 8, 1867, pg. 4, c. 6.

20 <u>Illinois State Journal</u>, Jan. 23, 1867, pg. 4, c. 4.

21 Ibid.

22 <u>Illinois State Journal</u>, Mar. 1, 1867, pg. 4, c. 3.

23 Plummer, "Governor, 1865-69," 24-25. <u>Illinois State Journal</u>, Oct. 9, 1867, in Plummer, "Governor, 1865-69," 24.

24 <u>Peoria Daily Transcript</u>, Apr. 15, 1868, pg. 2, c. 1, pg. 3, c. 2. Plummer, "Governor, 1865-69," 28-29.

25 Plummer, "Governor, 1865-69," 30-32.

Chapter 3

State Dining Room.

Governor Shelby M. Cullom.
Photo courtesy of the Illinois State Historical Library.

1869-1901: Republican Ascendancy

The steady progression of Union army veterans into the Executive Mansion continued when John M. Palmer was elected governor in 1868. Palmer was born in Kentucky in 1817, but his father disliked slavery and moved the family to Illinois in 1831, settling near Alton. Palmer attended Shurtleff College, then sold clocks and taught school before turning to the law in 1839. He moved to Carlinville, where he married Malinda Ann Neely in 1842. She bore him ten children during a forty-three-year marriage.[1]

Palmer was a man of great independence, perhaps to the point of being mercurial. During the Civil War, he rose from colonel to major general, serving with distinction until he abruptly resigned his command after a dispute over precedence of rank in 1864. Upon becoming governor, Palmer quarreled with his own political party–the Republicans–vetoed bills by the bushel, and sniped at the corruption of President Ulysses S. Grant's administration. He placed great emphasis on affirming state rights, a philosophical outlook associated in the popular mind with the defeated Southern Confederacy. He soon migrated into the Democratic party.[2]

Malinda Palmer suffered from poor health for much of her life. She had contracted the dread scourge of tuberculosis. The war years were particularly difficult for her as she struggled to raise her large family with her husband away serving in the army. She wrote him plaintive letters, expressing her great desire for his safe and prompt return home. Her distress was compounded by illness among her children; epilepsy afflicted a son, Tom, blindness, an infant daughter, Susie. Palmer encouraged Malinda to patiently endure her troubles, but his worry and concern over the health of his wife and family contributed to his decision to resign his wartime command. "Offices and honors are very unsatisfactory things when the little ones are afflicted," Palmer wrote.[3]

Mrs. Malinda Ann Neely Palmer thought herself too provincial to be first lady.

Photo courtesy of the Illinois State Historical Library.

As Palmer's political star ascended and he began to emerge as a credible candidate for governor, Malinda worried that she lacked the polish and sophistication to be first lady. "A woman that has stayed at home as much as I have would not make a very stylish wife for the governor," she fretted. Palmer naturally encouraged his wife, but her poor health prevented them from entertaining in the Executive Mansion beyond the receptions that duty required. Malinda was uncomfortable in Springfield and longed to return to Carlinville. When she died in 1885, Palmer mourned her deeply. Five years after they had married, Palmer had written her: "I would my wife if it would not seem foolish for me . . . tell you how much I love you and how I long to hold you in my arms. I am . . . a Husband but none the less a Lover four years have rubbed down the harsh points

Governor John M. Palmer.
Photo courtesy of the
Illinois State Historical Library.

Mrs. Julia Fisher Cullom.
Photo courtesy of the
Illinois State Historical Library

in the character of us both and I know our love for each other burns as bright as on our marriage day." She had been a child bride in an age when that was permissible, and he had been both husband and father to her.[4]

Palmer and the Republican party had fallen out of love with each other as his term drew to a close. He did not run for reelection, giving as his reason that he could not support Grant at the top of the ticket. Republicans tapped the ever-popular Richard Oglesby again, and he was elected by a wide margin. Soon after, the state legislature elevated Oglesby to the United State Senate, and Lieutenant Governor John L. Beveridge was sworn in as Oglesby's replacement on January 23, 1873. Five days later fire consumed the colossal home Governor Joel Matteson had built across the street from the Executive Mansion, its fiery demise heralding the end of that sad chapter in Illinois' history.[5]

The most notable event in the Mansion during Beveridge's tenure was the visit of President Ulysses S. Grant in October 1874. Grant had come to dedicate the Lincoln Monument in Oak Ridge Cemetery, and he was the guest of Governor Beveridge at the Executive Mansion. After the ceremonies at the tomb, a glittering reception for the president was held at the Mansion. Grant seemed to enjoy himself, though his typically emotionless demeanor betrayed few clues. Also of note was the birth of a baby girl, the daughter of Beveridge's son Philo and his wife Ella Rutzer, in the Executive Mansion on the morning of October 31, 1874. The Illinois State Register reported that she weighed ten pounds, and that her father "treads the earth with the pride of a war horse." The proud parents named their daughter Kühne, which means "daring," and she became a prominent sculptor, whose subjects included Grover Cleveland, Buffalo Bill, and King Leopold of Belgium.[6]

Beveridge aspired to another term, but he was bested in the Republican primary by Shelby M. Cullom, who went on to win the general election. Cullom had lived in Springfield for many years, and his ascension to the Executive Mansion pleased local citizens. His family consisted of his second wife, Julia Fisher Cullom, who was the sister of his deceased first wife, and two daughters, Ella and Carrie, children of his first marriage. While Cullom was governor, the state legislature appropriated $9,000 for refurbishing the Executive Mansion. Two years later, in 1883, the legislature provided $1,000 for a new roof and improvements on the chimneys and fence.[7]

Cullom was the first governor to win a second term, he was reelected in 1880, but he was elected to the U.S. Senate and resigned before completing his second term. His six years in the Mansion witnessed the visit of another president of the United States. Rutherford B. Hayes had been elected in the controversial election of 1876, in which Hayes lost the popular vote to Democrat Samuel Tilden but was awarded the office by a commission appointed to sort out the electoral mess. Critics called Hayes "His Fraudulency," while his frail wife Lucy's devotion to the temperance cause–she refused to serve alcohol in the White House–earned her the sobriquet "Lemonade Lucy."

"His Fraudulency" and "Lemonade Lucy" arrived in Springfield at the Alton depot early on the morning of September 30, 1879. Traveling with the president was General William T. Sherman, hero of the Atlanta campaign, coiner of the memorable and pithy phrase, "War is hell." Hayes's visit was graced by a beautiful fall day, the sky was robin's egg blue, and the sun glinted off the shiny scabbards of the militia units assembled to meet the presidential party. The Rockford Rifles and the Governor's Guard escorted Hayes and company to the Executive Mansion, where the president and his wife were given a hearty breakfast and an hour or two of rest before the "official" reception at the State Capitol. Later in the morning the presidential party departed for the Capitol grounds as the Springfield cannon battery fired a twenty-one gun salute, the loud reports prompting the horses to shiver with fright in their harnesses. The Capitol was gaily decorated for the presidential visit, the entrance marked by three arches festooned with evergreens, a symbol of eternal life. Each arch bore a sign. One read "Welcome to the Capitol of Illinois," while the other two read "Lincoln" and "Douglas," respectively, reminding the visiting dignitaries of honored favorite sons. Speeches of welcome were given by state and local officials, and Hayes and Sherman responded with appropriate remarks. Then it was off to the fairgrounds, and more speeches. Mrs. Hayes, wearing a plain black dress as befitting her sober public image, was presented with a silver and crystal epergne (an ornamental fruit dish) by the Women's Christian Temperance Union. The president and his party then had lunch at the "No. 1 Dining Hall," the food prepared by the women of St. Paul's Episcopal Church. A tour of the fairgrounds and the Lincoln Monument followed before the tired guests were shepherded back to the Mansion for supper.[8]

Governor Richard J. Oglesby, "Uncle Dick", as an honored veteran of the Civil War.

Photo courtesy of the Illinois State Historical Library.

Governor Cullom wanted to give ordinary citizens an opportunity to meet the president, so he scheduled a public reception at the Mansion from 8 to 11 p.m. that evening. Excited crowds engulfed the Mansion at 7 p.m., and throughout the three-hour period throngs packed the receiving line. Mrs. Hayes had exchanged her widow's wear for a cream white silk dress that was decorated with lace and pearls. Her jewelry was studded with diamonds and onyx. She and the president dutifully pumped hands and greeted the masses before surrendering to fatigue and retiring to a guest bedroom at 10 p.m. General Sherman soldiered on until the official closing hour of 11 p.m., demonstrating again the fortitude for hard campaigning that had served him and the Union cause so well in the late war. The local newspaper sardonically noted that a gang of pickpockets staked out the Mansion's entrance where the immense crowd bunched up as it entered, and the thieves lifted a rich harvest of watches and wallets.[9]

In 1882 the Executive Mansion was the site of a wedding reception for the governor's daughter Ella, who married William Barrett Ridgely. The ceremony began at 6 p.m. and was conducted at the First Presbyterian Church, the governor escorting his daughter down the aisle in the time-honored fashion. Ella's wedding gown of ottoman silk was characterized as "chaste and elegant." Afterwards the guests repaired to the Mansion, where the bridal party greeted them in the east parlor, next to a bay window decorated with ivy, smilax, and white flowers. The Mansion's parlors were also decorated with tastefully arranged flowers. Supper was served in a room adjoining the east parlor, the repast a creation of Kinsley of Chicago, a respected caterer. An orchestra from the local watch factory entertained, and many tried to dance to the fine music, though they found it difficult in the crowded parlors.[10]

When Cullom was elected to the Senate in 1883, his lieutenant governor, John M. Hamilton, became governor and completed the final two years of Cullom's term. Hamilton was thirty-five years old when he moved into the Executive Mansion, and he had a graduate degree from Ohio Wesleyan University. He was younger and better educated than most of his predecessors. Hamilton wanted to run for governor in his own right in 1884, but the Republican party chose the reliable vote-getter Richard J. Oglesby, who went on to win his third nonconsecutive term as governor. He and his second wife, Emma Gillett Keays Oglesby, came to the Executive Mansion, familiar surroundings for Oglesby.[11]

Within months of Oglesby's return to office, the state legislature passed a substantial appropriation for the Mansion: $4,000 was earmarked for a kitchen addition, $1,000 for repairs to the driveway and sidewalks, $3,000 for painting and repairing the Mansion, stable, and coal house, and $3,000 for a fence enclosing the grounds. In addition, $23,600 was provided to pave the streets and build new sidewalks around the Mansion.[12]

Mrs. Oglesby was the daughter of John D. Gillett of Elkhart in Logan County, a self-made millionaire, the "Cattle King" who raised prize stock and corn. Emma appreciated the finer things in life and imbibed the Anglophilia of her social set.

Window of Mansion. It is of the original style from Chicago architect John M. Van Osdel.

Some of the upper strata of society consciously imitated English manners, fashions, and customs. The Springfield papers carried news from England on all these subjects. Readers could digest articles headlined "England's Young Men: What Shall the Upper Classes Do With Their Sons?" and "The Briton's Imperturbability." An account of Lady Randolph Churchill, the former Jenny Jerome of New York City, described her organizing English women into the Primrose League, a grass-roots Conservative women's group whose members canvassed door to door.[13]

Emma was a member and financial contributor to the Episcopal Church. While the children of other governors attended local public schools, Emma's children were educated

Emma Gillett Keays Oglesby and son Jasper, August 1888.

Photo courtesy of the Illinois State Historical Library.

at home by a governess, who conducted her "classes" in a room that the children remembered was near the cupola in the Mansion. Personal attention produced well-mannered children. Young Felicite Oglesby greeted a new acquaintance with the salutation, "I am very glad to meet you." The Oglesby children were given a pony and cart in which to ride about, and the cart was characterized as an English type.[14]

Emma Oglesby's fondness for all things English extended to her manner of entertaining at the Mansion. She was a fine hostess and enjoyed staging parties, often with a particular theme. An air of formality typified many events, as written invitations were sent to select guests. The parties often had English themes. For example, a Dickens party had all the guests dressed as characters from the popular novels of the English novelist, Charles Dickens. One young girl at the time remembered being forced to wear pantalettes, much to her chagrin, in imitation of a character from the novel <u>Nicholas Nickelby</u>. Perhaps most interesting was Mrs. Oglesby's celebration of Twelfth Night, the feast of the Epiphany, that honored the Three Wise Men who followed the star to find and then worship the baby Jesus. Though steeped in Christianity, the festival had medieval overtones. In England, a large cake was baked, called the Twelfth-Cake, and a bean was placed inside. Pieces were distributed to the party guests, and whoever recovered the bean was named king for the day and won the title King of the Bean.[15]

Mrs. Oglesby's version of Twelfth Night was a fund raiser for the St. Paul's Parish Aid Society. A large Twelfth

Night cake was baked with pounds and pounds of raisins that had been laboriously pitted in the church rectory by the ladies of the society. The program for the evening at the Mansion went as follows: first, costumed children performed "vocal lancers," then they recited nursery rhymes, then Mrs. Oglesby directed Moore's dance, performed by masked children. Finally, the massive fruit-filled cake was borne out by "stout pages." Since it was a fund raiser for the church, adults paid a fifty-cent admission fee, while children were twenty-five cents. Coffee and cake were twenty-five cents, while each additional piece of cake was fifteen cents and another cup of coffee was ten cents.[16]

Just before the end of his term, Governor Oglesby's daughter Olive ("Ollie") married Chester A. Snider of Hannibal, Missouri, at St. Paul's Episcopal Church, with a reception afterwards at the Executive Mansion. Springfield society had anxiously awaited this winter wedding–they were married on December 28, 1888–as a welcome distraction from the gray dreariness of the season. Snider was a businessman who had a young daughter from a previous marriage. He met Olive at a wedding in Omaha in September, the two experienced love at first sight, and a rapid courtship followed.[17]

The wedding ceremony was conducted in the evening. Olive wore a beautiful gown, a diamond necklace, and garlands of fresh hyacinth. Her bridesmaids carried diminutive bouquets of roses trimmed with white gauze and pearls. The church was crowded with guests; visitors from Chicago chartered special railroad cars for the occasion. A reception for the multitude followed at the Executive Mansion, with Colonel William L. Distin of the Illinois National Guard acting as master of ceremonies. Other members of the National Guard assisted Colonel Distin in his social duties, probably organizing the receiving line among other things. Their dress uniforms, sparkling with gold braid and brass, added a bit of pomp, as the guests enjoyed sumptuous food prepared by the oft-used caterer Kinsley of Chicago. Mr. and Mrs. Snider received gifts of silver, rare china, and leather-bound books, then romantically decamped on the midnight train for a two-week honeymoon.[18]

Joseph W. Fifer survived a near-fatal bullet wound and became governor of Illinois.

Photo courtesy of the Illinois State Historical Library.

Oglesby's successor, Joseph Fifer, was yet another Civil War veteran and Republican. Fifer was a Bloomington attorney who had been the state's attorney in McLean County, and had served in the state senate. During the Vicksburg campaign,

Fifer had been gravely wounded in battle near Jackson Mississippi. He was hit in the chest, the ball penetrating the right lung and liver. He was shipped back home to Bloomington to die, his recovery considered an impossibility. Yet, miraculously, Fifer survived, earned a degree from Illinois Wesleyan, studied law, and was admitted to practice.[19]

His wound continued to plague him. He was a gaunt, sickly man who was often unwell. By sheer force of will, he performed as a trial lawyer before juries, collapsing with fatigue afterwards. His daughter Florence remembered hearing on countless occasions the solemn pronouncement "he can't live through the year," from local physicians. But Fifer lived on and prospered in the demanding trade of trial lawyer, drinking buckets of coffee to keep going.[20]

In a strange manner, Fifer's terrible wound led to his election as governor. Fifer had been granted a pension of twenty-four dollars per month because of the severity of his wound, based on an act of 1883, which permitted that amount for a pensioner whose disability was equivalent to the loss of an arm or a leg. Incredibly, John C. Black, the Democrat Commissioner of Pensions, claimed in congressional testimony that Fifer's pension had been increased for political reasons. Fifer published a savagely effective response to Black's charge, in which he unfavorably compared Black's war record and character to his own. His letter was noted in important Republican political circles, and Fifer found himself drafted to run for governor, running as "Private Joe" Fifer, an allusion to his simple military rank. The campaign taxed Fifer's perilous health. He recalled that "the physical suffering I endured was beyond belief." Fifer gave speech after speech and ended each arduous day in a "miserable" hotel "with hot bricks at my feet and blankets piled over me as I shook near nervous collapse." He defeated former governor John M. Palmer, now a Democrat, by over 12,000 votes.[21]

"Private Joe" Fifer and his wife Gertrude and their two children Herman and Florence found a well-supplied Executive Mansion thanks to outgoing Governor Oglesby, who had generously refilled the Mansion's coal supply and had offered to leave his cow for the governor-elect's family. Fifer was inaugurated as governor on January 14, 1889. He was forty-eight years old, and his daughter described him as "tall and handsome, with coal black hair

Gertrude Lewis Fifer.
Photo courtesy of the Illinois State Historical Library.

and dark eyes." The new governor's children were quite opposite in character. While Herman was quiet and studious, Florence was a spoiled and boisterous tomboy whose mischievous behavior was constantly overlooked and excused by her adoring father. "She is an angel from Heaven. She can do no wrong," the governor would say when informed of her latest escapade. Her mother would always smile knowingly. The Fifers were permissive parents in an age that prized discipline for children. Florence and Herman were given substantial freedom.[22]

Not surprisingly, Florence acted up at the inaugural ball. "The great spiral staircase probably impressed me more than anything inside the mansion, as it would any child who

Florence Fifer.

*Photo courtesy of the
Illinois State Historical Library.*

loves sliding down banisters," Florence remembered. "The first opportunity to try it came the evening of the inaugural ball . . . To the shocked surprise of the guests, John Oglesby, son of the former governor, and I came shooting down the banister into the midst of the receiving line, scattering dignitaries right and left! My new white dress had a wide streak of dark gray straight down the front, but the banister was lustrous from the unaccustomed polishing." The governor and Mrs. Fifer, ever indulgent, laughed at Florence's rascality and permitted her to stay up for the ball.[23]

In May the state legislature provided $13,500 to remodel the Mansion, and the Fifers moved back to Bloomington for a few months while the work progressed. Gertrude Fifer was a popular first lady, but she was criticized for installing large glass panes in the bay windows of the east and west rooms. Purists claimed that this change ruined the Mansion's style. Gertrude was unconcerned by the criticism, and the remodeling bore her impress. "My mother, for all her quiet gentleness, knew what she wanted and in her tasteful way was always able to carry through," wrote Florence later. Gertrude disliked the numerous portraits of former governors which hung from the Mansion's walls, a somewhat macabre gallery of the dead. She took advantage of the remodeling to banish them to the governor's State House office under the pretext of protecting them from harm.[24]

Once back in the Mansion, Florence resumed her pursuit of amusement and mischief. Her bedroom was in the northeast corner, and she recalled a "beautiful rosewood bed . . . hung with a light satin canopy and lace curtains." But Florence was scarcely in her bedroom, as she spent every free moment on her most prized possession, a black pony she named Dixie. Governor Fifer had given his daughter the pony with an ulterior motive–he wanted Florence to stay off his prize Kentucky saddle horse. Florence devoted her young life to horseback riding. She practiced riding tricks over and over again, hoping to join the circus as a trick rider. Perhaps most memorably, Florence trained Dixie to climb the Mansion's steps and walk into the front hall, much to the consternation of the staff and unsuspecting visitors. Governor Fifer would simply watch bemused, though he would quickly chase horse and rider back outside. When the governor reviewed the state militia at their annual summer rendezvous, Florence rode beside him on Dixie. School paled in comparison to such adventures, and Florence took little interest in it, beyond expressing annoyance that it took her away from Dixie. "I . . . never read a book of my own free will until I was fifteen years old," she confessed later. She tried every dodge to be excused from class, preferring to be practicing tricks on Dixie.[25]

When not on her pony, Florence was getting into other forms of trouble. The Fifers kept a cow in the Mansion's barn for fresh milk. The barn was surrounded by an old stone wall, and Florence and her playmates would prance about the top of the wall frightening the cow until it stopped giving milk. A perplexed Governor Fifer was repeatedly forced to acquire new cows, all the while puzzling over what had upset the last. Florence and her friend Owsley Brown once jumped on a slow-moving freight train and took a ride through Springfield on the roof of a rail car. A flagman chased them away. Just off the state dining room was a glass enclosed porch with a fountain. Florence used the burbling fountain as the home for a pet baby alligator. Later, to keep the little alligator warm on a cold evening, Florence placed it in a basket and left it on a warm oven in the kitchen. The cook promptly baked the unfortunate creature to a crispy turn. "That incident was one of the major tragedies of my life at the mansion," said Florence. Given some of her stunts, one wonders if the cook acted deliberately.

Florence is the rider at right in this 1892 photograph.

Photo courtesy of the Illinois State Historical Library.

Florence's mother, Gertrude Fifer, remained unfazed by her daughter's antics, at least to outward appearances. A committed Unitarian, Gertrude was of a progressive mind-set who taught church school and played the organ into her late seventies. She enrolled Florence in the Unitarian Sunday School at the age of two. Gertrude was very fond of the works of Ralph Waldo Emerson, Henry David Thoreau, and William Ellery Channing. She was a pacifist who found hunting distasteful and spoiled Governor Fifer's plan to make his grandson a great hunter by reading the child works by the conservationist Ernest Seton Thompson. Gertrude enjoyed ice-skating, and would take the children to frozen lakes in the frosty cold of winter, to glide and pirouette merrily about. She was also an "exquisite housekeeper."[27]

Florence remembered that her mother "had great independence of spirit and quietly but firmly usually had her way." Governor Fifer had a mania for punctuality. He felt that to keep another person waiting was a form of robbery. To avoid incurring their father's wrath, the Fifer children were always on time. Mrs. Fifer refused to submit to the tyranny of the second hand, and came and went at her own pace, often keeping the governor standing around muttering darkly under his breath.[28]

Gertrude was an accomplished hostess who took pleasure in her new Springfield friends. "Her natural interest in people and democratic attitude toward all were invaluable traits in a first lady," Florence recalled. Gertrude had a passion for music, and she shared her enthusiasm with Mansion guests. "A good musician herself, she saw to it that the mansion guests were entertained with musicales given by leading performers

One of the Mansion's parlors when Florence Fifer was in residence. Note the portrait of Abraham Lincoln.

Photo courtesy of the Illinois State Historical Library.

of the day." Florence received voice training from Mrs. Ella Hinkle at her home on South Fourth Street, and she performed at church functions and for the Amateur Musical Club. The Mansion was the center of Springfield's social life. The carpets would be carefully covered with white canvas, music provided, and dances held. "The state dining room was used for many a gay cotillion, and I was allowed to stay up and enjoy it all," remembered Florence.[29]

Gertrude displayed a nimble touch as hostess when presented with those unforeseen developments that habitually occur at social gatherings. Governor Fifer invited groups of state legislators to dine at the Mansion when the legislature was in session, a common practice among governors. One legislator happened to weigh in at a mammoth three hundred and fifty pounds. He was so large he needed extra room at table, but providing such had to be done in a discreet manner to avoid offending his dignity. Mrs. Fifer placed a bogus place card next to him, with a fake name, then simply removed it when the "guest" failed to arrive, thereby giving her colossal friend more eating space without an explicit acknowledgement of the need.[30]

After leaving office, Governor Fifer was appointed to the Interstate Commerce Commission by Presidents McKinley and Roosevelt. The Fifers moved to Washington, and Gertrude took advantage of the many cultural delights of the East. She loved to browse the congressional library, delighted in the art galleries, and embraced the ebullient social life of the national capital. Gertrude endorsed women's suffrage, stating: "I am a firm believer in the equality of men and women. The virtues and vices of the sexes may differ in kind, but are very evenly balanced." Her mother's independent nature encouraged Florence to undertake her own political career.[31]

In 1924 Florence was elected as a Republican to the Illinois Senate, becoming the first female state senator. She had worked tirelessly to establish a tuberculosis sanitarium in McLean County, and this and other charitable activities, along with her famous name, had prompted local leaders to select her as a candidate. Her mother unreservedly supported her candidacy. "It was her faith that instilled in me the strong belief that whatever comes we always have the power to meet it," said Florence. Former Governor Fifer, perhaps recalling the sight of a rosy-cheeked little girl cantering a pony up the stairs of the Executive Mansion, remarked on his daughter's election: "I declare . . . and I didn't think she was worth educating." Florence served several terms before being swept out in the 1932 Democratic landslide.[32]

Florence Fifer Bohrer receives congratulatory handshakes from her mother and daughter after taking the oath as Illinois' first female senator, January 1925.

Photo courtesy of the Illinois State Historical Library.

Governor John P. Altgeld
at his cluttered desk, 1896.

*Photo courtesy of the
Illinois State Historical Library.*

Gertrude Fifer faced death with the same dignity with which she had faced the challenges of life. Florence was vacationing in Michigan when she received word that her mother was ill. She quickly returned home. Her mother greeted her calmly, though she was clearly failing. She asked the nurse to leave the room. She briskly informed her daughter, "Florence, I want you to promise not to do anything to prolong my life. I am not going to recover. I made up my mind last spring that the time had come for me to go. I've had a long life and an interesting one." Florence discovered that her mother had indeed made out her will the previous April. She lived another month before passing away. "Private Joe" Fifer became an elder statesman of the Illinois Republican party. He continued to be active, giving speeches into the 1930's. Remarkably, given the horrible wound he had sustained, Fifer lived until 1938, dying at the age of ninety-seven.[33]

Fifer was defeated for reelection as governor in the Democratic landslide year of 1892. His victorious opponent, John Peter Altgeld, was a taciturn, German-born lawyer and successful real-estate speculator and developer. Altgeld had campaigned hard, purportedly spending $100,000 of his own money in the effort. He became the first Democratic governor in Illinois since Joel Matteson.[34]

Born in Germany and raised in Ohio after his family emigrated, Altgeld suffered under a tyrannical father. He escaped for a time as a soldier in the Civil War, but he contracted an illness, perhaps malaria, that hampered him for the rest of his life. After the war, Altgeld left parental abuse behind and headed west for Kansas and Missouri where he worked as a teacher and manual laborer. He studied law and was admitted to the Missouri bar in 1871. After stints as a city attorney and county prosecutor, Altgeld suddenly moved to the booming metropolis of Chicago in 1875, where he made a fortune in real-estate speculation.[35]

In 1884 Altgeld published a book condemning the penal system. He suggested that poor environment produced criminals, and he advocated an emphasis on rehabilitation rather than punishment. He unsuccessfully competed for seats in the U.S. House and Senate and was finally elected to the Superior Court of Cook County in 1886. Six years later he was contending for the Executive Mansion.[36]

Altgeld's wife Emma Ford Altgeld was a graduate of Oberlin College, and a musician, painter, and writer. "She is tall and lithe and her carriage is one of natural grace," remarked a contemporary. The Altgelds had no children, an earlier pregnancy had tragically ended in a stillborn birth. So the Mansion halls that had once rung

Emma Ford Altgeld.

*Photo courtesy of the
Illinois State Historical Library.*

The southeast parlor and music venue during the Altgeld administration.

Photo courtesy of the Illinois State Historical Library.

with the peals of laughter and shouts and screams of Florence Fifer and her mischievous playmates were quiet now. Altgeld was a pensive man, rather humorless, renowned for his stone-faced demeaner. Still, the Altgelts entertained, fulfilling the social obligations demanded of a governor, and they found their place in Springfield society.[37]

Both Governor and Mrs. Altgeld enjoyed horseback riding for exercise. Vachel Lindsay remembered Altgeld being thrown from a horse on the Mansion grounds, then quietly mounting again with his famous stoic expression intact. Mrs. Altgeld rode sidesaddle, as was customary for women, and often donned a silk riding hat. Perhaps paradoxically, Altgeld enjoyed dancing, though his ability was questionable. One Mansion guest recalled watching the Altgelds as they "hopped about quite solemnly." A group of young Springfield men was allowed to use the Mansion drawing rooms for a series of balls, called the Springfield Assembly Balls. White canvas was placed on top of the Mansion carpets to facilitate

Jade vase and goblets. On loan from the Federal Government.

dancing. At one ball on November 10, 1893, Governor and Mrs. Altgeld greeted their guests in the northeast parlor. Roses and chrysanthemums added a splash of color on mantels and other pleasing nooks about the rooms. The program included fourteen dances accompanied by the local orchestra, which was located between the east and west parlors. Upon arrival, young ladies ascended the winding staircase to deposit their coats in the bedrooms, then gracefully descended to their waiting beaus, the young men attired in formal evening dress complete with white gloves. Refreshments were provided in the tearoom.[38]

Mrs. Altgeld was popular in Springfield women's circles. She often asked local friends to accompany her on horseback rides about the city, politely inviting them for lunch or a snack afterwards. She became an honorary member of the Springfield Women's Club and hosted Club functions at the Mansion throughout her tenure as first lady of Illinois.[39]

Altgeld served a stormy single term as governor. Exhausted from the campaign, he was too ill to finish his inaugural address to the state legislature, and he slumped into a chair, sick and feverish. He was forced to withdraw from public life for a time and recover his health. He governed as a liberal, raising property taxes and spending the surplus. Like Matteson, the last Democratic governor, he regarded the state treasury as a personal bank, borrowing $50,000 to prop up his failing real-estate investments.

Governor John R. Tanner.
Photo courtesy of the Illinois State Historical Library.

Friends reimbursed the state treasury. On June 23, 1893, he pardoned three men jailed for their involvement in the Haymarket bombing of 1886, a labor riot in which several policemen were killed. Altgeld's pardon was an eighteen-thousand-word manifesto that enraged his critics and reenergized his political opponents. His actions enabled Republicans to successfully tag him as a radical and a coddler of criminals early in his term. It was said that Altgeld's middle name was not Peter but "Pardon." John "Pardon" Altgeld could never shake the label, indeed his liberal activism as governor only reinforced it. Republicans retook the state legislature in 1894 and mounted a strong effort against his reelection in 1896. The campaign featured a "Flying Squadron" of former Republican governors touring the state on behalf of the Republican candidate, John R. Tanner. Altgeld was defeated. He died in 1901 shortly after delivering a speech in Joliet.[40]

John R. Tanner, Altgeld's Republican successor, had been a political workhorse for decades. He had served honorably in the Union army in the Civil War; his father and two brothers lost their lives in the conflict. He emerged from the army to begin a steady political climb in Clay County. He held many elective and appointive posts: sheriff, circuit clerk, state senator, marshal, assistant treasurer.

His most dramatic political victory prior to becoming governor was his 1886 election as state treasurer. He was an ambitious man, physically imposing with a massive moustache that covered his face, and he knew everyone worth knowing in Republican political circles.[41]

Tanner's inauguration as governor was preceded by a socially spectacular marriage to Cora English, a prominent and eligible young woman from a good Springfield family. Tanner's first wife had died in 1887, and he was left to raise two children. Cora had been educated in Springfield, then traveled abroad for two years as was fashionable among the children of wealth and good breeding.[42]

They were married at St. Paul's Episcopal Church in Springfield at noon on December 30, 1896. The church was still festively decorated for Christmas, with holly, evergreens, and bells of red immortelles. Twelve hundred invitations had been sent out, the church was packed, and some had to stand for the service while an interested crowd of spectators waited outside. In the crush of guests, former governor John Palmer was bumped by "ragamuffins" and nearly knocked to the ground. He was unable to get into the church and went home. Two minutes before noon, Governor-elect Tanner and his best man arrived, and the throng about the church cheered as they leapt from their carriage and dashed around to a side entrance. Close on their heels came the bride and her father in a magnificent landau with blue leather seats, pulled by a team of nut-brown Kentucky mares. The landau was a gift from political supporters in Cook County. The crowd again applauded as Cora's father assisted her out of the carriage and escorted her into the church. Her wedding gown was of mirror velour and all white, while lilies of the valley adorned her shoulders and the front of the gown. She was popularly considered the most beautiful woman in Springfield, and she certainly appeared so on her wedding day.[43]

Cora English Tanner.
Photo courtesy of the Illinois State Historical Library.

The ceremony was described as unostentatious, a testimony to the bride's good taste and the groom's good sense. Outside, boys propped a ladder on a dry-goods box and peered through stained-glass windows, witnessing a service conducted in the "old English style." The bride's diminutive niece, little Edith English Buck, known as "Cricket," acted as flower girl. She wore a blue silk gown and carried a basket of forget-me-nots. At the conclusion of the ceremony, the happy couple walked past row upon row of smiling friends and relatives to emerge from the sanctuary as Mr. and Mrs. Tanner, to the delighted cheers of the crowd.[44]

A reception for a select few was held at the residence of Cora's father on South Sixth Street. Amidst the roses, palms, and tropical plants that decorated the house, the fortunate invitees dined on quail on toast, chicken salad, green peas, and potatoes. A nine-piece orchestra conducted by Louis Lehman entertained with selections of light opera. In the late afternoon, the Tanners departed for a honeymoon to the south, traveling in a lavishly

appointed railroad car that was staffed with a cook and porter. Unfortunately, their honeymoon was cut short as political disputes compelled Tanner to return to Chicago.[45]

The Capitol was elaborately decorated for Tanner's inauguration, scheduled for January 11, 1897. Thousands of lights were strung about the dome, a spectacular one hundred evergreen wreaths, and miles of drapes, silk banners, and colorful crepe paper provided a brilliant backdrop of colors. The east entrance was draped in an immense flag nearly two hundred feet long. After being sworn in, the governor and Cora went to their new home, the Executive Mansion, to dress for the inaugural ball.[46]

The Tanners were not pleased with the condition of the Mansion. They found a dingy and run-down building with cracked plaster, peeling paint, and leaky faucets. The spiral staircase that had been Florence Fifer's plaything was near collapse. The gas-powered lights did not function properly–Cora was forced to dress for the ball to the uncertain light of guttering candles. As she donned her evening gown of white moiré, with pearls and a sparkling diamond tiara for adornment, Cora decided to champion the renovation of the Mansion. Her husband was given to extravagance, and he readily embraced the project.[47]

On January 20, 1897, Speaker of the Illinois House Edward C. Curtis of Kankakee appointed a special committee to investigate the condition of the Executive Mansion. Committee members inspected the Mansion on at least two occasions. The committee report, issued at the end of April, painted a sorry picture. A foul stench drifted up from a broken sewer in the basement. A steam boiler was worn to the point of being unsafe. Paint peeled on interior and exterior walls. Furniture was obsolete and falling apart. The floor, worn from countless social events, was sunken in spots. Woodwork, railings, and steps were rotting; the roof leaked. The committee concluded that the Mansion was in a "deplorable condition" and recommended that $30,000 be appropriated for a complete renovation. The recommendation was referred to the appropriations committee.[48]

On June 10, 1897, the Illinois General Assembly approved $27,241 for the facelift of the Mansion. The money was earmarked as follows: $3,766 to repair the basement, $300 for plastering, $3,000 for repairing plumbing, bathrooms, and sewer, $1,480 to construct a brick and stone boiler house, $2,500 for a steam heating apparatus, $1,500

Pitcher, bowl, and soap dish. Antique set acquired to complement the Bartels Collection.

for a new grand stairway and interior wood finish, $3,000 for interior painting and decorations, $475 for outside painting, $6,125 to put copper roofs on the Mansion and cupola, $1,500 for a copper balustrade, $315 for an attic floor and woodwork on the cupola, $3,500 to place a stone and granite porch and marble steps on the north front, and $780 to repair the sidewalks and build additional walks on the Mansion grounds. To conduct this ambitious renovation, the Tanners hired Springfield architect George Helmle, who was designing and building the homes of Springfield's elite. Helmle's sons George and Henry worked on the project too. The Tanners moved into a suite at the Leland Hotel while the renovation proceeded.[49]

Herman Meyer was a German-born sculptor commissioned to carve the Illinois State Seal into the Mansion's portico as part of the Tanner renovation in 1897. Meyer is shown above next to the seal. He holds the simple wooden maul with which he worked. Born in Prechtal, Germany, Meyer was trained in a carving school and emigrated to Farmer City, Illinois, in 1891. He moved to St. Louis and worked for the Culver Stone Company. Shown at the right, Meyer's state seal. Unfortunately, Meyer's beautiful seal did not survive the renovation of 1971-72. His work can be viewed at the New Cathedral in St. Louis, at which Meyer carved the pulpit and baptismal font.

Photo courtesy of Lorin I. Nevling.

The result was dramatic, as the Mansion was re-created as a residence of which to be proud. Outside, the single flight of steps on the north side where Florence had ridden Dixie up and into the Mansion was demolished. A portico replaced them, with two flights of steps to the east and west. A bas-relief of the state seal was chiseled from stone and located where the two flights of steps joined at the porch. A mansard roof was constructed with a balustrade and flagpole on top of it, and the old cupola was enclosed.[5]

Inside, the winding staircase was removed and replaced by a stairway similar in design to stairs in France's renowned Fontainebleau Palace. The newel post of dark, rich mahogany was offset by white spindles, and gold leaf was sprinkled on the baseboard. The stair rail and white spindles ringed the balcony upstairs that led to the sleeping quarters. An orchestra was located there during social events. Corinthian pillars, white with gold leaf, were placed in the hall. In Cora Tanner's favorite room, the northeast reception room, the walls were covered in pink tapestry. The artist Kiestner painted cupids carrying rose garlands on the ceiling, tranquil cherubs gazing down at mere mortals. Governor Tanner's office was to the left of the entrance; to the right was a billiard room. Two new coatrooms were built so that guests might deposit their coats before gliding up the stairs to a social event.[51]

Equally important but less glamorous changes were made. The Mansion's plumbing was tied into the city water supply. Prior to this change, the Mansion had been supplied from an attic water tank, the water hand pumped into it from cisterns. More bathrooms were possible with the new abundant water supply. Servants too now had their own bathroom, although Mrs. Tanner was disappointed to discover that the servants kept mops and buckets in the bathtub rather than use it as intended.[52]

On the east side, a music room was finished in white woodwork. Silk tapestry covered the walls, while the carpet was white with gold scrolls, a reproduction of carpeting at the Fontainebleau Palace. A northeast drawing room was decorated in green tapestry. A breakfast room featured red tapestry walls, oak paneling, and a beautiful blue ceiling. The state dining room was finished in forest green tapestry and wood paneling. Cora placed a six-foot-tall Venetian cut-glass cabinet in this room. The cabinet had an enamel cupid in the center of the upper panel, and its sides were covered with rose garlands and forget-me-nots.[53]

The Executive Mansion had been reborn in the fashion of the end of the nineteenth century, a mixture of dignity and opulence, of beauty and gaudiness. Cora Tanner was credited with the result, and she won much praise for the successful outcome. Her husband warned her to relish the moment of glory, as he knew the fickle nature of public opinion.[54]

The Tanner Cadets stand in front of the newly renovated Executive Mansion in 1898.

Photo courtesy of the Illinois State Historical Library.

The new Mansion quickly became the headquarters for Cora Tanner's many social events: teas, open houses, dinners, receptions. Among the famous who visited the Mansion were President William McKinley, James Whitcomb Riley, Tanner's friend "Buffalo Bill" Cody, and the famed female shootist, Annie Oakley. The first New Year's open house following the renovation, the Tanners kept the Mansion open all day and into the evening, greeting countless callers from all social classes curious for a look at the improvements. Refreshments were served in the state dining room and the breakfast room. Holiday decorations, smilax, evergreen, mistletoe, and Christmas bells enchanted the multitude, who enjoyed ices and cakes served by Mrs. Tanner's friends. The Tanners unpretentious attitude earned the moniker "democratic Republicans."[55]

As governor, Tanner accomplished some needed reforms, notably establishing a pardon board, championing a child labor law, and achieving election reforms. However, he had become enamored of election to the U.S. Senate. Rather than pursue a second term as governor, he fought the incumbent senator, former governor Shelby Cullom, for the Senate seat. Perhaps Tanner's ambition was a product of a visit he and Cora made to Washington early in their term to witness William McKinley's inauguration. Cora Tanner had made a splash in Washington society; her beauty had been remarked upon in the local press. Unfortunately for Tanner, Cullom rather effortlessly fended off his challenge and retained his Senate seat. Tanner's failure seemed to shake his health. He became ill in May 1901 in the wake of a trip to New York. Confined to his suite at the Leland Hotel, Tanner sank rapidly and died on May 23, 1901, with Cora at his side. His tomb in Oak Ridge Cemetery is a massive granite temple, an extravagant memorial to an extravagant man. Cora lived another forty-five years before joining him in death.[56]

Five cherubs in garden.

Endnotes

1 George Thomas Palmer, <u>A Conscientious Turncoat: The Story of John M. Palmer</u>, 1817-1900 (New Haven: Yale University Press, 1941), 1-3, 5-11, 14-15.

2 Robert P. Howard, <u>Mostly Good and Competent Men</u> (1988; reprint, Springfield: University of Illinois at Springfield, 1999), 126-31.

3 Palmer, <u>Turncoat</u>, 214.

4 Ibid., 137-38, 227-28.

5 Octavia Roberts Corneau, "The Governor's Mansion, 1853-1953," 47-48, Octavia Roberts Corneau Collection, ISHL. <u>Illinois State Journal</u>, Jan. 29, 1873, pg. 4, c. 3.

6 Corneau, 49-50. <u>Illinois State Register</u>, Oct. 31, 1874, pg. 4, c. 1. "Kühne Beveridge," <u>Journal of the Illinois State Historical Society</u>, vol. 23 (July 1930), 325-27.

7 Corneau, 54. <u>Illinois Laws</u>, 1881, 38; 1883, 45.

8 <u>Illinois State Journal</u>, Oct. 1, 1879, pg. 2, c. 1-2, pg. 3, c. 6.

9 <u>Illinois State Journal</u>, Oct. 1, 1879, pg. 2, c. 1-2, pg. 3, c. 6.

10 <u>Illinois State Journal</u>, Oct. 25, 1882, pg. 6, c. 1-2. Corneau, 58-60.

11 Howard, 149-151.

12 <u>Illinois Laws</u>, 1885, 21-22, 35.

13 <u>Illinois State Journal</u>, Jan. 7, 1886, pg. 7, c. 1, pg. 6, c. 1, Jan. 6, 1886, pg. 7, c. 1.

14 Corneau, 66-67.

15 Corneau, 67-70. Richard J. Oglesby Scrapbook, 1886-87, Oglesby Papers, ISHL.

16 Illinois State Journal, Jan. 3, 1886, pg. 8, c. 3, Jan. 5, 1886, pg. 8, c. 1, Jan. 7, 1886, pg. 8, c. 4.

17 Illinois State Journal, Dec. 28, 1888, pg. 1, c. 7.

18 Ibid.

19 Fifer's wound described in report to regimental surgeon and affidavit to War Department in Fifer-Bohrer Collection, ISHL.

20 Florence Fifer-Bohrer, "Memoirs," 4-5, Fifer-Bohrer Collection, ISHL.

21 Joseph W. Fifer to Editor, <u>Chicago Inter-Ocean</u>, Apr. 27, 1886, in Fifer-Bohrer Collection, ISHL. Fifer-Bohrer, "Memoirs," 171. Howard, 374.

22 Oglesby to Fifer, Springfield, Jan. 9, 1888, in Fifer-Bohrer, "Memoirs," 10-11, 12, 1-2.

23 Fifer-Bohrer, "Memoirs," 12-13.

24 Ibid., 23-24. <u>Illinois Laws</u>, 1889, 20-21.

25 Fifer-Bohrer, "Memoirs," 13, 25, 77, 14. Corneau, 76-77.

26 Fifer-Bohrer, "Memoirs," 13-16.

27 Ibid., 16-17, 7, 77, 89, 119.

28 Ibid., 3-4, 13.

29 Ibid., 22-23, 67, 26.

30 Ibid., 24.

31 Ibid., 70, 123.

32 Ibid., 124, 127, 145.

33 Ibid., 118.

34 Howard, 160.

35 Ibid., 160-62.

[36] Ibid., 161.

[37] Henry Barnard, Eagle Forgotten: The Life of John Peter Altgeld (1938; reprint, Secaucus, N.J.: Lyle Stuart, Inc., 1973), 57-58. Corneau, 90-91. Illinois State Journal, Jan. 1, 1897, pg. 4, c. 3-4.

[38] Corneau, 88, 90-91. Waldo R. Browne, Altgeld of Illinois: A Record of His Life and Work (New York: B.W. Huebsch, Inc., 1924), 67-68. Illinois State Journal, Nov. 10, 1893, pg. 4, c. 1.

[39] Corneau, 89. Illinois State Journal, Jan. 1, 1897, pg. 4, c. 3-4.

[40] Howard, 165-66. Illinois State Journal, Jan. 8, 1897, pg. 4, c. 2.

[41] Howard, 187-88.

[42] Ibid., 188.

[43] Illinois State Journal, Dec. 30, 1896, pg. 2, c. 3, Dec. 31, 1896, pg. 2, c. 4-5.

[44] Illinois State Journal, Dec. 31, 1896, pg. 2, c. 4-5.

[45] Illinois State Journal, Dec. 31, 1896, pg. 2, c. 4-5, Jan. 3, 1897, pg. 3, c. 4.

[46] John T. Trutter and Edith English Trutter, The Governor Takes a Bride (Carbondale: Illinois State Historical Society and Southern Illinois University Press, 1977), 14-15.

[47] Corneau, 97-98. Trutter, 53.

[48] Illinois House Journal, 40th sess., Apr. 27, 1897, 671-73, 10, 17, 78.

[49] Illinois Laws, 1897, 16-17. Trutter, 57.

[50] Corneau, 99-100, Trutter, 57-58.

[51] Trutter, 57-58.

[52] Corneau, 99.

[53] Trutter, 58-59.

[54] Trutter, 59.

[55] Trutter, 70. Illinois State Journal, Jan. 2, 1898, pg. 5, c. 1-2.

[56] Trutter, 60.

Chapter 4

*Garden looking down
from the east porch.*

Governor Yates, standing far left, welcomes President Theodore Roosevelt to the Mansion. Roosevelt is the fourth from the left. Seated in front are Catharine Geers Yates, the governor's mother, and Helen Wadsworth Yates. *Photo courtesy of the Illinois State Historical Library.*

1901-1921: A New Century

Richard Yates II was the living embodiment of that wretched historical cliché, the transition figure. The first governor who had been born in Illinois, he entered office at the beginning of the twentieth century while personally remaining a prisoner of the nineteenth. He was the son and namesake of the governor who presided over state government during the Civil War. That conflict haunted the son, as it had tormented and ultimately destroyed the father. At his inauguration, Yates's visions were not of the future, but of the past. As he watched a military parade march through the Mansion grounds, the color drained from his face in vivid recollection. Mrs. Yates noticed. "Richard, you look as if you have seen a ghost." Yates turned to face her. "I don't know but that I have; the ghost of many marching feet." And then he remembered rows of neat, blue-clad regiments marching in review as he stood as a boy on the Executive Mansion's porch. His father, the governor, was weeping unashamedly beside him from a combination of bourbon and remorse at sending young men to their deaths. Yates could not shake these melancholic reveries, which became more immediate when he moved into the Executive Mansion.[1]

The past collided awkwardly with the future in the Yates administration. He entered office with a prominent and bushy mustache, a nineteenth-century fashion, but abruptly shaved it off early in 1901, embracing the new clean-shaven look. Yates had a large military staff, as had many of his Civil War veteran predecessors, earning much newspaper criticism for employing ostentatious but useless colonels. A devout Methodist, Yates had watched helplessly as alcoholism destroyed his father; the experience made him an abstainer, so he was in sympathy with the growing prohibition movement. "I had been taught to renounce the devil and all his works, including Old John Barleycorn," he recalled. Yates cultivated a public image of strict probity and acted accordingly as governor. At a time of much government reform and activism, he was obsessed with paring state spending. "The practice of prudent economy in the conduct of the affairs of the State government was one of the important features of my administration. In pursuing this course I was obliged to disregard my own personal interests," Yates recalled. He gave as an example his veto of a $15,000 appropriation for the improvement and repair of the Executive Mansion. Yates even vetoed spending he had recommended to the state legislature![2]

Yates and his wife, Helen Wadsworth Yates, had two daughters, Cathcrine, age nine, and Dorothy, age five. Dorothy made a splash at the 1901 inaugural ceremonies when she tired of her father's speech and began shouting for him to stop reading and take her home. Grandmother Yates calmed Dorothy, fluttering her fan to distract her. The family moved into the imposing Executive Mansion, and Mrs. Yates quickly began to make her mark.[3]

Helen Wadsworth Yates.
*Photo courtesy of the
Illinois State Historical Library.*

Helen Wadsworth Yates was a great asset to her husband who, though a youthful forty, struggled with the mental and physical demands of the governor's office. Contemporaries noted that Mrs. Yates seemed "fitted by education, training and distinguished lineage" to become first lady. She was related to the famed Wadsworth family, who counted the poet Henry Wadsworth Longfellow among their number. Helen was educated at Illinois Women's College, and had been active in women's clubs in Jacksonville, where she and Richard made their home after their 1888 marriage. She possessed a "generous nature," tact, intelligence, and perhaps most importantly, strength to bear up under the pressure of events. The social duties required of a governor's wife were arduous–the unending stream of guests, the receptions and dinners–rarely would Mrs. Yates have an evening alone with her husband for four years. She was devoted to her cherubic spouse, and she wore her wedding gown at the evening reception following his inauguration, a testament to her affection for him. She was characterized as "democratic" in manner, able to converse with average folks, but her Wadsworth blood enchanted the more aristocratic doyennes of the powerful Daughters of the American Revolution. She seemed a woman for all seasons.[4]

An article in the local newspaper described the appearance of the Executive Mansion during Mrs. Yates's tenure. The Mansion was "a perfect type of an old-fashioned English country place," with "well kept lawns," "spacious drives," a vast Edenic expanse studded with imposing oak trees. The Yates girls, "flaxen-haired children," roamed the grounds, playing hide and seek with local kids, shouting and shrieking with delight at the discovery of a friend hiding in the hedges. Mrs. Creer, a family servant for many years, tried to teach the children croquet with mixed results. While chaos reigned outdoors, Mrs. Yates put her imprimatur upon the Mansion's interior. The staircase was painted black and its carving gilded. She closed the fireplaces in two rooms and concealed them with large mirrors. A "cozy corner" was created at the point where the

The Illinois Executive Mansion when Richard Yates was governor.
*Photo courtesy of the
Illinois State Historical Library.*

A holiday receiving line at the Executive Mansion. Mrs. Yates and the governor are at left.

Photo courtesy of the Illinois State Historical Library.

stairs descended from the main hall to the basement. There she placed a couch with canopy and side curtains, an elaborate nook where a guest could catch his or her breath.[5]

The governor held weekly receptions for state legislators during the legislative sessions, and Mrs. Yates helped render those events a success. She was charming and facile in conversation and could cope with the conversational transitions demanded in a state that sent both hog farmers and bankers to the State House. Informality characterized those events, putting everyone at their ease. Mrs. Yates also held weekly afternoon receptions as first lady, called "At Homes," and these were a bit more formal in character. Typically, women with positions in society were the attendees. Mrs. Yates appeared at these gatherings in regal dress, and spoke like the well-educated and well-traveled woman that she was. "She discussed the latest book, the newest style, the current topics of the day and indulges in the unimportant small talk of such occasions." Mrs. Yates clearly dominated Mansion events, leading some observers to conclude that she made more political friends on social occasions than the governor and his aides. Mrs. J. H. Strong was certainly impressed. "She is altogether one of the nicest women I ever met.

She is gifted in a variety of ways, but I think her chief charm is her unaffected and sincere manner. She is interested in people, and she shows it in a hearty way."[6]

Colorful flowers and understated elegance distinguished the decoration of the Mansion in the Yates years. When Mrs. Yates staged a benefit for the Home for the Friendless, the Mansion "was aglow with pretty lights. Everywhere they shone in happy brilliancy. Clusters of roses and chrysanthemums were effectively arranged about the rooms. Smilax, ferns and palms also were used to complete the decorations." Mrs. Yates seems to have been fond of pink. She was described at one gala as "a glorious vision in pink, very deep pink, like the darker tint of a sea shell. Her gown, her hat, and her muff were all of the same shade, and the gown was trimmed in quantities of big silk roses the same color of pink." Mrs. Yates was a patron of the arts, and music was often featured at her receptions. She helped launch the career of Carrie Jacobs Bond by inviting her to perform at the Mansion. Bond, whose hits included "I Love You Truly," became a renowned songwriter.[7]

Mrs. Yates needed all her innate strengths when Governor Yates contracted the dreaded typhoid fever in the fall of 1902. Yates had embarked on a strenuous campaign for Republican candidates in early October. He gave countless speeches, often several in a day, and exhausted his health. Yates became ill and stammered through an October 25 speech at Cairo. Forced to return to Springfield on October 26, he collapsed into bed. His

A Yates rally at the Mansion's north entrance.

Photo courtesy of the Illinois State Historical Library.

physician, Dr. L. C. Taylor, was called and found that the governor had a high fever, over 103 degrees. His condition gradually worsened, and on October 29, Dr. Taylor diagnosed Yates with typhoid fever.[8]

Yates had a morbid fear of typhoid fever, now virtually unknown, but a great killer in the nineteenth century, particularly of children. As a boy, the governor had endured an attack of typhoid, as had his brother Henry and sister Katie. Henry's son died from the disease. Worried that learning the true nature of his sickness would inhibit his recovery, Helen Yates told the governor he had "intermittent fever," not typhoid. She was constantly nursing him in the weeks that followed, endangering her own health. Two nurses eventually were hired to assist her. Yates's severe fever caused him to slip into delirium, and his manic, unintelligible cries were painful for Helen to witness. While Yates lay feverish, his private secretary, John Oglesby, himself the son of a governor, tended to the duties of the office.[9]

Fireplace in the Library.

No one except the doctor and members of the Mansion household were allowed to see the governor. The Mansion gates were closed, vehicles prohibited on the grounds, and the Yates daughters sent to school in Jacksonville. There was considerable speculation on the governor's condition, the propriety of John Oglesby acting in his stead, and how Helen Yates was holding up under the strain. On November 8, Dr. Taylor reportedly ordered Mrs. Yates to rest and to allow the nurses to look after her ailing husband. Sickly with fatigue, Mrs. Yates recovered quickly after sleeping, but was more inclined to let the nurses tend to the governor.[10]

It was a long siege. Not until November 18, three weeks after the onset of the disease, did Governor Yates show signs of improvement. On that morning he awakened and requested a breakfast of corn cakes. The doctor thought corn cakes were too much for him in his weakened condition, but at Thanksgiving the governor was allowed to have a bit of turkey. On December 1, 1902, the iron gates of the Mansion creaked open and vehicles were again allowed on the grounds. A little over a week later, Yates and Helen left for Florida to recuperate, at the doctor's suggestion. Yates was so frail and emaciated he had to be carried on board the train for Miami, and Dr. Taylor came along to look after his famous patient. He recovered and successfully completed his term.[11]

Yates's successor, Charles S. Deneen, had been state's attorney in Cook County, at which he had earned plaudits for socially diverse prosecutions of bankers and murderers. Deneen immediately set the tone for his administration at his 1905 inauguration, which was sober, not a gala bash. His young daughter Dorothy was ill in Chicago with appendicitis, which naturally tempered enthusiasm. However, beyond that personal worry, the sober tone was in keeping with Deneen's preference. There was no "thoughtless rejoicing." Deneen held no inaugural ball and refused to serve liquor at the Mansion. The National Guard and its glittering officials, who cost Yates so much grief, were banished from the inaugural parade. Deneen's address was characterized as "business-like," with no "wasted space or spreadeagle-ism or political glorification." Deneen

Governor Charles S. Deneen.
Photo courtesy of the Illinois State Historical Library.

was a clean-shaven man who did not drink, and he entered office with a fixed reform agenda. Normally he did not wear a hat, but it was expected attire for the inaugural ceremony. Forced to repeatedly doff his hat in salute, Deneen struggled. The Chicago Tribune reported: "It was a perfectly good hat . . . but it stuck. It would not come off easily, and when it was on it was always liable to come off. Therefore, the new governor's progress through the halls of the statehouse was marked by a series of wretches and jerks at his headgear that would greatly have perturbed any ordinary man." Reaching the podium near which sat the Deneen family, the governor-elect noted that his young son Ashley winked at him. Ever dignified, Deneen did not respond in kind.[12]

After attending a luncheon at the Hotel Leland, Deneen and his wife Bina boarded a train and rushed back to Chicago and their daughter Dorothy. They found her in good spirits if not health, proud of her father the governor. Soon after, Dorothy's appendix was removed. The family delayed moving into the Executive Mansion until Dorothy could travel. The state legislature appropriated $12,000 to repair and refurnish the Mansion for the Deneens.[13]

Deneen's wife, Bina Day Malony, was from Mount Carroll, Illinois, where her father farmed. She acquired her education at the Frances A. Shimer Academy and became a member of the First Methodist Episcopal Church. The Deneens had four children, Charles Ashley, Dorothy, Frances, and Bina. Charles Ashley was a lovable scamp who started each day by kissing a bust of Lincoln at the base of the stairs. Bina, the youngest, was born in 1906, while Mrs. Deneen was in Michigan on vacation. The Mansion staff doted on the baby, who delighted everyone.[14]

Mrs. Deneen was a popular first lady who maintained an arduous schedule both at the Mansion and in Chicago. "How mother ever managed the continuous round of entertaining, I can't imagine, except for her youth, her genuine affection for the people (whether political friends or not), and her unselfishness towards her children," recalled her daughter Dorothy. Mrs. Deneen was a polished society woman who was quite comfortable at glittering receptions or exclusive club meetings. She dressed immaculately in a manner that she believed befitted her station. For example, as the guest of honor at a 1909 Chicago luncheon hosted by the Tuesday Art and Travel Club, Mrs. Deneen wore "a beautiful gown of olive green silk, gold lace and cream white threaded with gold." She sported a prominent black hat that featured colorful plumes.[15]

Mrs. Deneen brought her exquisite taste to the decoration of the Mansion. Her artful touch was evident on New Year's Day in 1909. Beautiful carnations, ferns, palms, and smilax splashed the home with color, giving guests a pleasant whisper of spring and summer amidst the spartan chill of January. Visitors were received in the east reception room, which had been smothered in pretty green smilax, it was even draped on the chandeliers, giving the effect of entering a peaceful bower. Ferns, smilax, and palms were artfully placed throughout the west drawing room and library, and both rooms featured an arrangement of carnations, simple but elegant. The main hallway was decorated with azalea plants, stevia blossoms, and the ubiquitous ferns and palms. The main dining room was radiant, with bowls of roses and baskets of poinsettias and ferns on tables, red candles in the candelabra, and magnolia leaves "arranged in a sort of frieze about a plate rock." An Illinois State Register correspondent concluded: "The decorations at the mansion were beautiful and attracted more than passing attention."[16]

Governor Deneen served two terms in the Executive Mansion and hoped to win a third. Theodore Roosevelt's decision to run a quixotic third party campaign for president in 1912 divided the Republican party in Illinois and the nation. As a result, Democrat Edward F. Dunne was elected governor in 1912. Dunne was the first Catholic since William Bissell and the only former mayor of Chicago to be elected governor. Though a staunch Democratic partisan, Dunne had remained somewhat aloof from the political machines that dominated the party in Cook County. He was known for his devotion to his large family, and he exuded a comforting middle-class respectability. His marriage to the former Elizabeth F. Kelly has been described as a "love match." The Dunnes had thirteen children, though sadly only nine survived by 1913. The Dunne children were Edward Jr., Eileen, Mona, Maurice, Richard, Jerome, Eugene, Jeannette, and Geraldine.[17]

After the election, Governor and Mrs. Deneen invited the Dunnes to visit the Executive Mansion, their new home for the next four years. Mrs. Dunne openly wondered if her large brood could fit in the Mansion. "Why, I was startled when I found . . . there were just six sleeping rooms. One of these . . . is the state or guest room. . . So with a room for Mr. Dunne and myself there remained . . . only four for the use of our children." Somehow the Dunnes would have to fit, and they removed their children from Chicago schools in anticipation of their move to Springfield. Unfortunately, a protracted battle to choose a speaker for the Illinois House delayed the inauguration ceremonies, originally

Mrs. Bina Deneen and baby Bina.
Photo courtesy of the Illinois State Historical Library.

scheduled for January 12, to February 3. The four youngest Dunne children, Jerome, Eugene, Geraldine, and Jeannette, frolicked about their Chicago home, released from classroom discipline. "They have been out a whole month now, and are simply running wild," a harried Governor-Elect Dunne confessed to a reporter. "I don't know what they will do when they have to pin themselves down to their books again."[18]

Finally, the Illinois House chose a speaker, and the arrangements for Dunne's swearing in were completed. Mrs. Dunne organized the move to Springfield with assistance from her two daughters, Eileen and Mona. The family packed and trundled along six suitcases and eight trunks, one trunk for each child who would be living in the Mansion. "The most trouble, as usual, was with the boys' trunks," said Mrs. Dunne. "They bring the most impossible things to pack. Ball bats, velocipedes, roller skates, aeroplanes and what not. All at the last moment, too. The girls were bad enough with their dolls. They wanted them packed just so, of course." Several hundred books from Dunne's vast personal library, each one painstakingly marked with chalk, would be moved later.[19]

The Dunnes managed to reach Springfield, which was covered in a thick winter blanket of snow, where they took up residence briefly at the St. Nicholas Hotel. A reporter sent to interview the new first lady found conversation nearly impossible as the

Paper cutouts from 1860-1870.

Stuffed porcelain doll 1860-1879. The head and shoulders are porcelain. The body is kid leather with sawdust or horse hair.

Dunne children raced about the room, banging on a piano when not banging on each other. Dunne was sworn in at noon on February 3, 1913, a ceremony marked by a remarkable degree of amity between Dunne and outgoing governor Charles S. Deneen. The two men had been friends for more than twenty years. After the swearing in, the new governor and his family repaired to the Mansion for a luncheon with a select group of family and friends.[20]

Two carriages delivered the children from the State House to the Mansion, where they approvingly surveyed the immense snow-covered grounds. "Gee, what a dandy place to play Indian," nine-year-old Eugene enthused. "Yes," agreed his brother Jerome. "This is big enough for a football game." Entering the Mansion, the little Dunnes gazed wide-eyed at the cavernous reception rooms, the artwork, and the glittering chandeliers.

The Executive Mansion as it appeared when Governor Deneen was in residence. *Photo courtesy of the Illinois State Historical Library.*

The Dunne family, standing (left to right): Mona, Eileen, Edward, Mrs. Dunne, Maurice and Richard. Seated: Eugene, Governor Dunne, Jeannette, Mrs. E. F. Dunne, Jr., Geraldine, Robert Jerome. *Photo courtesy of the Illinois State Historical Library.*

The boys soon discovered the billiard room and began smacking the balls around, while Geraldine, Jeannette, and their mother retired for naps. "It's a fine boarding house," laughed the new governor.[21]

That evening Governor and Mrs. Dunne held a public reception from 8 to 11 p.m. at the Mansion. Democrats were naturally enthused at retaking the governor's office after a long drought, and an estimated three thousand people clogged the receiving line. The new governor was tired and looked it, but he stood his ground and pumped hands in a rose-colored drawing room decorated with baskets of pale roses, carnations, and the ever-present smilax. Clad in an evening gown of black moiré with diamond jewelry, Mrs. Dunne proudly stood with her husband for nearly three hours. The sheer numbers overwhelmed the cloak room, and many guests were forced to greet the governor and first lady clad in winter coats and galoshes, much to their chagrin. Not until after midnight did the receiving line finally dwindle out. The next day Mrs. Dunne found it difficult to open and close her right hand. The governor was also hand-sore, and a physician treated both. Shaking thousands of hands was both laudable and painful.[22]

The following day, Dunne went to his office in the State House for the first time and met informally with reporters. After disposing of political topics, the questioning turned to the Dunne family. What were they doing on their first full day in the Executive Mansion? "My little daughter Jeannette had to have a sled when she got a look at the mansion grounds," the governor reported. "Consequently she has been spending much time today sliding down the slopes in the yard." Young Eugene had made his father promise before the election that if elected, he would celebrate by giving him a pony. "Now, the boy is trying to hold me up in fulfillment of that promise," Dunne smiled. He also announced that he and his family would become members of Springfield's Church of the Immaculate Conception. The state legislature approved $16,000 to improve the Mansion for the large Dunne brood.[23]

Children's tire swing in the east gardens.

There was intense curiosity about the new first lady, who had so many children, and newspapers rushed to provide their readers with a profile. Mrs. Elizabeth Dunne was different from her recent predecessors. The demands of her large family had left her little time to be a member of women's clubs, as was fashionable. Governor Dunne chuckled that she was president of the "Home Club." Tall, with thick dark hair that was showing hints of gray, and an engaging smile, Mrs. Dunne described herself as a "home woman." She left the political world to Governor Dunne. "I always try to keep away from the discussion of politics," she told one reporter. "I find that I can do more good in my work as a mother and a wife." Though the Dunnes had a cook for nineteen years, Mrs. Dunne took special interest in the kitchen, and on occasion she would personally prepare a pie or favorite dish for her husband. She was gentle and caring with the family's servants. "I have always made it a point to be a friend of those who help me in the running of the house, to sympathize with them, to be interested in their affairs and to treat them as one of my own." The children were of course a special concern, and Mrs. Dunne kept a well-stocked dispensary to treat their ailments, from fevers to scraped knees.[24]

Mrs. Dunne's confinement to the domestic realm did not mean she lacked opinions or was necessarily reticent about expressing them. As the Illinois State Journal put it: "The fact that she has looked after the wants of thirteen children and a husband has not narrowed her mental vision." Governor Dunne credited his wife and the stable and loving home environment she provided with his success. For her part Mrs. Dunne felt that her large family was attractive to voters, noting that President Theodore Roosevelt's many children had garnered much favorable press coverage. Though reluctant to speak out, when pressed she advocated women's suffrage, if in a tentative manner. "I have never given much attention to the subject, but I think if the women want it they should have it–probably," she told a reporter. Although Governor Dunne ultimately signed a women's suffrage bill and boasted of it, he had never publicly supported it out of fear of alienating Chicago's powerful liquor interests, who worried that women voters would vote to prohibit liquor–as they soon did.[25]

Whatever her preference for home life, Mrs. Dunne soon embarked on the social duties required of her station as the governor's wife, aided by her two daughters Eileen and Mona. On the evening of March 26, 1913, a reception for General Assembly members was held at the Mansion. Roses, ferns, and palms decorated the rooms, and each room had a particular color theme. Yellow was the color for the state dining room, white and green for the library. The Dunnes also made their debut into Springfield society. Miss Leonore Hippard hosted a tea at her Second Street home for Mona and Eileen to introduce them to young people in their age group. The Dunne girls reciprocated with a dinner party at the Mansion, the tables ornamented with beautiful spring daffodils. The local Republican establishment made its peace with the new governor, who accepted invitations to dine at the homes of former governor Richard Yates and the widow of former governor Richard Oglesby.[26]

The Dunnes clearly embraced their roles as host and hostess for the state of Illinois. They entertained a number of distinguished guests, including William Jennings Bryan and former presidents Theodore Roosevelt and William Howard Taft. Dunne later recalled with some humor his manner of dealing with the thorny issue of prohibition at dinner parties. Those who supported prohibiting liquor were called "drys," while those who opposed prohibition were called "wets." No prohibitionist himself, Dunne habitually offered his guests a before-dinner cocktail. "I always announced that the drys should accompany Mrs. Dunne to the parlor of the mansion where she served them with grape juice; while the wets should accompany me to the library where I served them with a little something more inspirational," Dunne remembered. To the governor's vast amusement, the "wet" legislators went with Mrs. Dunne, while the "dry" legislators went to the library for a whiskey![27]

Though the Dunnes entertained former presidents and other high officials, their most pleasant Mansion function was their daughter Eileen's wedding reception. Eileen Dunne and William Joseph Corboy had been childhood sweethearts. After Bill graduated from Yale and became an attorney in the Dunne family law firm, he proposed and Eileen accepted. The newspapers called their romance an "old fashioned love affair," and praised Eileen's "simplicity of character." The wedding was set for the morning of October 20, 1915, at

A Teddy Bear created and named for President Teddy Roosevelt from a newspaper account of a bear hunt in Mississippi. His refusal to shoot an old bear that beaters had flushed and wounded captured public sentiment. 2002 is the 100th anniversary of "Teddy's bear".

The Corboy-Dunne bridal party at the Executive Mansion. Newlyweds William and Eileen Corboy are at the foot of the steps, left.

*Photo courtesy of the
Illinois State Historical Library.*

the Church of the Immaculate Conception in Springfield. The Very Reverend Timothy Hickey, the vicar general of the Alton diocese and a man known for giving couples blunt marital advice at the altar, was to marry the pair.[28]

Early that day Governor Dunne was pacing around the Mansion, smoking a cigar "furiously," just another anxious father on his daughter's wedding day. An estimated two thousand people packed the church for the 10:30 a.m. ceremony. Eileen had requested that security around the Mansion be relaxed so members of the public could enter the Mansion grounds and see the wedding party. Dunne brothers and sisters were actors in the ceremony. Mona Dunne, the bride's sister, was matron of honor in a pink satin dress with matching pink slippers. Eugene and Jeannette Dunne were ring bearers. The bride wore a spectacular gown and carried a bouquet of lilies of the valley. Old and wizened, Father Hickey did not disappoint, admonishing the bride and groom "not to both talk to each other at once." This remark drew a smile from Mrs. Dunne, who had been weeping steadily since her daughter made her appearance in the sanctuary. With rough good humor, Hickey told the bridegroom to focus on his home life. "Don't join clubs like a bachelor, but make your club at home," he said.[29]

Governor Frank O. Lowden.
Photo courtesy of the Illinois State Historical Library.

After the service, the bridal party returned to the Executive Mansion for photographs on the steps leading to the main entrance. Guests soon joined them for a memorable breakfast reception. The Mansion was described as presenting "a fairy-like scene of beauty." The east drawing room featured pink roses draped on the mirrors and garlands of smilax on the ceiling and walls. The library and music rooms were decorated with bouquets of white chrysanthemums. The state dining room was graced by a massive three-tier wedding cake with little sugar cupids, doves, and hearts. Four wedding bells of roses hung over the bridal table. The reception continued until 3 p.m., at which point Mr. and Mrs. Corboy had to prepare to depart on their honeymoon. It had been an enchanting day.[30]

Dunne served a single term and his successor was Republican Frank O. Lowden, another Chicago-area attorney. Lowden was married to the fabulously rich Florence Pullman, daughter of George M. Pullman, controversial owner of the Pullman Company. They met in 1894 on board a

Florence Pullman Lowden.

Photo courtesy of the
Illinois State Historical Library.

ship bound for Europe, and the pair later shared a romantic tour of Paris. Lowden was smitten, and he won Florence's hand. He then had to overcome the resistance of her formidable father, a man known for his explosive temper. This took time. Eventually, the lovers won his consent, and Frank and Florence were married on April 29, 1896. They had four children: Florence, Frances, Pullman, and Harriet. Lowden relentlessly pursued his legal career, unwilling to be submerged as the husband of a Pullman heiress, and he was drawn into Republican politics. In the end, he was elected governor in 1916, on the eve of American entry into the First World War.[31]

Florence Lowden had been raised in an opulent world that would have been foreign to most of her contemporaries. She was educated at the most elite academies in Chicago and New York, and in Europe at Fountainebleau and Potsdam. She traveled across the country in a luxurious railroad car with her father, who doted on her. She was familiar with the kind of social whirl typical of a first lady's tenure at the Executive Mansion–teas, receptions, dinner parties, charity benefits and dances. Her family wintered at an estate in Florida, summered on the St. Lawrence River, and made annual pilgrimages to Europe. Her wealth, good breeding, culture, and social prominence led to expectations that her years in the Mansion would be the most glorious in its history.[32]

Yet Florence Pullman Lowden did not relish the role of first lady. Never in particularly robust health, she worried that the social demands of a term in the Executive Mansion would overwhelm her. She thought the political world rather vulgar, a man's world that refined women should avoid. Her attitude was not snobbish, merely a simple and understandable reluctance to enter the fish-bowl political world, where a private life often becomes impossible. She was horrified when Frank left the world of law and business for a political career, but her love for him and sense of duty made her adapt. During Lowden's gubernatorial tenure, Mrs. Lowden accompanied him on countless trips to dusty small towns, sweaty county fairs, and muddy army camps, shook the hands of thousands of common folk, and all with good humor and grace. She had great discernment with regard to proper interior design, skills she brought to her renovation of the Mansion. She conducted her social events with grace and style, and Springfield embraced her. Mrs. Lowden became a member of the Springfield Women's Club, YWCA, the local chapter of the Daughters of the American Revolution, and the First Presbyterian Church.[33]

Just three months into Governor and Mrs. Lowden's tenure, the United States declared war on Germany and entered the First World War. Lowden now became a war governor, with greater responsibilities. Any display of social high life at the Mansion was out of the question. The Lowdens were expected to lead the Illinois war effort by example, and because of their privileged background they were under great press scrutiny for any misjudgment. Governor Lowden never cared much for dinner parties and receptions, so their absence was no great hardship for him. Plunging into mobilization, he was soon known as "Win the War Lowden" for his propensity to judge every policy question in terms of its effect on the war effort. Mrs. Lowden and her daughter Florence were active in the Red Cross and other war-related charitable organizations. Her diary records almost daily visits to the local Red Cross office, and she was always knitting war items, such as a rifle mitten. She judged knitting contests, and urged the purchase of Liberty Bonds. They had "wheatless" teas to set an example of sacrifice, and daughter Florence gave lectures on the importance of conservation.[34]

The Lowdens found the Executive Mansion in poor condition, with a rodent and insect problem, a leaky roof, ancient plumbing and lighting, and dilapidated furniture. "It is difficult to heat this big house satisfactorily with the present old fashioned equipment," Mrs. Lowden noted in her diary. Governor Lowden was always prone to colds, and they plagued him in the drafty Mansion. Taking the matter in hand, Mrs. Lowden consulted a Chicago contractor for estimates on a substantial renovation. She wanted to give the Mansion a more home-like feel, and with this in mind she added an awning to the porch and installed new flowerbeds. In July 1917 the main renovation work began, and the Lowdens moved into the home of John W. Black on Williams Boulevard. Mrs. Lowden supervised the work, visiting the Mansion often to give suggestions to the contractor. The renovation was finished in October, and the Lowdens moved back. The project cost nearly $50,000, of which the Lowdens paid roughly half, with the state government paying the other half.[35]

The Executive Mansion during the Lowden administration.

Photo courtesy of the Illinois State Historical Library.

Mrs. Lowden gave Nellie Brown Duff, a reporter for the <u>Illinois State Journal</u>, a tour of the remodeled Mansion. The first lady was quick to describe the latest facelift as simple and unostentatious, as merely putting the Mansion in good order. She stressed that necessities were updated–the heating, plumbing, and lighting. This was a shrewd characterization tailored to the stark fact that the United States was involved in a European war. Trumpeting a grand remodeling would have been politically disastrous, unpalatable to a public called upon for sacrifice. Duff seemed convinced that the repairs were not frivolous, calling them "necessary and permanent improvements" that would last for years. [36]

More than necessities had been tended to, as the Mansion under Mrs. Lowden's touch became more "home-like." Specifically, she successfully lightened the atmosphere with brighter and more cheerful colors. In the main reception room to the left of the entrance, heavy, dark-red brocaded material was removed from the walls, which were then painted a deep cream. The white walls set off the mahogany furniture and woodwork, while rose curtains were retained, as they matched the upholstery of the furniture. A large mirror that had completely concealed a fireplace, with mantelpiece topped by a smaller mirror, added a homey touch. Mrs. Lowden retrieved a spectacular glass chandelier from the State House for the crowning touch.[37]

The state dining room had been "gloomy" with dark paneling and walls, providing a somber backdrop for state dinners. Mrs. Lowden changed the paneling and trim to mahogany, and decorated the room with green and white wall hangings. She replaced

all the furniture, substituting mahogany furnishings including a simple yet elegant buffet. A mahogany mantelpiece sported light green enameled brick and above it rose a portrait of Colonel Edward D. Baker, Lincoln's friend and fellow lawyer, martyred in the Civil War.[38]

The family dining room was brightened, the formerly black walls painted in cream and soft medium blue. Velvet door hangings, window overdrapes, and furniture coverings were also a matching blue. Mrs. Lowden did little to alter the living room, which had been previously remodeled, beyond having it done in the same light and cheerful manner. Governor Lowden favored an etching by Millet, *The Wood Cutter*, and this was placed above the mantel. The family's quarters were done up in white too, while the furniture was covered with cretonne, the same pretty material of which the curtains and drapes were made.[39]

The basement had been dark and forbidding without curtains or hangings, simply a dungeon of dark wood. Guests arriving by carriage entered the Mansion through this gloomy basement, and the first lady was anxious that their first vista of the governor's residence be pleasing and inviting. She had the black wood painted white and added red rugs and furniture coverings, a cheerful contrast from the previous motif. Governor Lowden's office was to the immediate left of the basement entrance, and its dark tone matched the surroundings. Mrs. Lowden had the wood painted white, the walls a light green, and covered the windows with white curtains and green drapes. The billiard room across the hall received a similar overhaul. Down the hall were two dressing rooms, one for each of the respective sexes. The ladies room was done in white, with new curtains and dressing tables, while guests could hang coats and hats on new, modern racks, which replaced an aging set of lockers.[40]

The reporter, Duff, concluded that the changes were "very much for the better," and she congratulated Mrs. Lowden for a remodeling of "quiet simplicity and charm." The Mansion now nicely fulfilled its dual role of site for state functions and home for the governor and his family. On October 30, members of the state cabinet and their wives had dinner at the Mansion and were suitably impressed by its new look. "The dinner last evening was very pleasant and the guests enthusiastic over the changes made in the Mansion," Mrs. Lowden recorded in her diary. In addition to partially funding the remodeling, Mrs. Lowden generously donated personal furniture to the Mansion. The items included an onyx pedestal, silk overcurtains, a Persian rug, and a gold-finished floor lamp.[41]

Endnotes

1 Richard Yates II, "Autobiography," 2-3, 18-19, Yates Family Collection, ISHL. Octavia Roberts Corneau, "The Governor's Mansion, 1853-1953," 108-109, Octavia Roberts Corneau Collection, ISHL.

2 Yates, "Autobiography," 113, 116-17, Yates Family Collection, ISHL. Olney Republican, [no date], Bound Volume 17, Yates Family Collection, ISHL. Corneau, 107, 109. Hillsboro News, Nov. 24, 1899, "His Mustache Shaved: Gov. Yates Presents a Great Altered Appearance," Illinois State Register, Mar. [17], 1901, BV 17, Yates Family Collection, ISHL.

3 Yates, "Autobiography," 135, 138, Yates Family Collection, ISHL.

4 Yates, "Autobiography," 135-39, Yates Family Collection, ISHL.

5 Chicago Daily News, Apr. 10, [1901], BV 17, Yates Family Collection, ISHL. Corneau, 113-14.

6 Chicago Daily News, Apr. 19, [1901], Mrs. J. H. Strong in undated clipping, BV 17, Yates Family Collection, ISHL

7 Undated clipping, BV 17, Yates Family Collection, ISHL. Illinois State Journal, undated clipping, BV 17, Yates Family Collection, ISHL. Yates, "Autobiography," 140-42, Yates Family Collection, ISHL. Corneau, 114-15.

8 Unknown newspaper clipping, Oct. 27, 1902, [State News], Oct. 28, 1902, Chicago Tribune, Oct. 27, 1902, Illinois State Register, Oct. 30, 1902, Illinois State Journal, Oct. 30, 1902, BV 19, Yates Family Collection, ISHL.

10 [State News], Oct. 29, 1902, Illinois State Register, Dec. 2, 1902, Illinois State Journal, Nov. 6, 12, 19, 1902, [Republic], Nov. 9, Springfield, Nov. 8, 1902, [Chicago Record Herald and Review], Nov. 10, 1902, BV 19, Yates Family Collection, ISHL.

11 Chicago Post, Nov. 19, 1902, [State News], Nov. 19, 1902, Illinois State Journal, Nov. 27, 28, Dec. 8, 1902, Illinois State Register, Dec. 2, 1902, BV 19, Yates Family Collection, ISHL.

12 Chicago Tribune, Jan. 8, 10, 1905, Springfield, Jan. 9, 1905, Mildred Conrad Horner Collection, ISHL. Illinois State Register, Jan. 17, 1909, BV 39, Charles S. Deneen Papers, ISHL

13 Corneau, 117-18. Chicago Tribune, Jan. 8, 22, 1905, Mildred Conrad Horner Collection, ISHL. Illinois Laws, 1905, 20.

14 Corneau, 119-20. Notes, Mildred Conrad Horner Collection, ISHL

15 Corneau, 119, 124-25. Illinois State Register, Feb. 4, 1913, pg. 5, c. 7. "Governor's Wife Guest at Luncheon," Chicago Tribune, Jan. 27, 1909, BV 40, Deneen Papers, ISHL.

16 Illinois State Register, Jan. 2, 1909, BV 39, Deneen Papers, ISHL.

17 Richard Allen Morton, Justice and Humanity: Edward F. Dunne, Illinois Progressive (Carbondale: Southern Illinois University Press, 1997), 1-3, 12-15, 40. Edward F. Dunne, Illinois, the Heart of the Nation, 5 vols. (Chicago: Lewis Publishing, 1933), 2: 317-18. John D. Buenker, "The New-Stock Politicians of 1912," Journal of the Illinois State Historical Society, vol. 62 (Spring 1969), 35-52. "Governor Dunne and His Family," Illinois State Journal, Feb. 4, 1913, pg. 3, c. 2-6.

18 Dunne, Illinois, 2: 317-18. Corneau, 125. Illinois State Register, Feb. 2, 1913, pg. 2, c. 3-4.

19 Illinois State Register, Feb. 2, 1913, pg. 2, c. 3-4.

20 Illinois State Register, Feb. 3, 1913, pg. 2, c. 2-4.

21 Illinois State Register, Feb. 4, 1913, pg. 4, c. 4-6.

22 Illinois State Journal, Feb. 4, 1913, pg. 4, c. 1-2. Illinois State Journal, Feb. 4, 1913, pg. 6, c. 3-5; Feb. 5, 1913, pg. 7, c. 1-2. Dunne, Illinois, 2: 318.

[23] Illinois State Journal, Feb. 5, 1913, pg. 7, c. 1-2. Illinois Laws, 1913, 95.

[24] Illinois State Journal, Feb. 4, 1913, pg. 6, c. 3-5; Mar. 9, 1913, pg. 8, c. 1-5. Illinois State Register, Feb. 4, 1913, pg. 4, c. 7.

[25] Illinois State Journal, Mar. 9, 1913, pg. 8, c. 1-5; Feb. 3, 1913, pg. 2, c. 2-4. Morton, Dunne, 77-78.

[26] Illinois State Journal, Mar. 27, 1913, pg. 9, c. 3; Mar. 28, 1913, pg. 8, c. 1; Apr. 1, 1913, pg. 9, c. 1; Apr. 22, 1913, pg. 9, c. 2; Mar. 26, 1913, pg. 9, c. 3.

[27] Dunne, Illinois, 370.

[28] Illinois State Register, October 21, 1915, pg. 1, c. 3-4, pg. 2, c. 1-7.

[29] Ibid.

[30] Ibid.

[31] William T. Hutchinson, Lowden of Illinois: The Life of Frank O. Lowden, 2 vols. (Chicago: University of Chicago Press, 1957), 1: 40-44, 46-51.

[32] Ibid, 42.

[33] Ibid., 250, 61-62, 372, 242, 260-61, 76, 370.

[34] Ibid., 327-28, 366-71. Florence Pullman Lowden Diary, Apr. 4, 7, 9, 12, 13, 20, 23, 1917; May 17, 21, 25, 1917; June 4, 19, 1917; July 12, 21-23, 1917; Aug. 3, 6, 7, 21, 23, 1917; Mar. 5, 1918, Corneau Collection, ISHL. Florence Lowden Miller Journal, Apr. 3, 5, 1917; June 24, 1917; Oct. 23, 1917; Dec.14, 1917; Jan. 16, 17, 19, 21, 1918; Feb. 14, 1918; Mar. 5, 1918; Apr. 8, 1918, Corneau Collection, ISHL.

[35] Hutchinson, Lowden, 119, 370-71. Florence Pullman Lowden Diary, Jan. 11, 12, 14, 19, 23, 1917; Feb. 1, 2, 4, 1917; Mar. 23, 1917; Apr. 10, 1917; May 15, 26, 1917; June 20, 1917; July 2, 6, 1917; Aug. 1, 28, 1917; Sept. 5, 12, 17, 19, 25, 28, 1917; Oct. 1, 8, 9, 10, 17, 23, 24, 25, 30, 31,1917; Dec. 19, 1917, Corneau Collection, ISHL. Illinois Laws, 1917, 159.

[36] Illinois State Journal, Nov. 4, 1917, part two, pg. 1, c. 1-5. Hutchinson, Lowden, 370.

[37] Illinois State Journal, Nov. 4, 1917, part two, pg. 1, c. 1-5.

[38] Ibid.

[39] Ibid.

[40] Ibid.

[41] Ibid. Florence Pullman Lowden Diary, Oct. 31, 1918, Corneau Collection, ISHL. Personal Property Inventory, Sept. 1, 1920, Office of the Auditor of Public Accounts, Illinois State Archives. Frank O. Lowden to Len Small, Chicago, Jan. 10, 1921, Len Small to Frank O. Lowden, Springfield, Jan. 12, 1921, Illinois Executive Mansion Restoration, Illinois State Historical Library.

Chapter 5

Overview of the east gardens. Relatively new, they were established in the late 1980's.

Governor Len Small.

Photo courtesy of the Illinois State Historical Library.

1921-1949: "Normalcy," Depression, War

Though the First World War had much circumscribed society events, the tenure of Governor and Mrs. Lowden had nonetheless been an exciting one for Springfield society. Mrs. Lowden, heir to the Pullman fortune, had pitched wholeheartedly into volunteering for the war effort, to the delight of Springfield citizens. Imagine finding yourself at the local Red Cross office knitting rifle mitts next to the Pullman heiress! The war also contributed a welcome sense of unity and urgency that lent an exciting air to the capital city.

A formal receiving line at the Mansion, probably for New Year's Day. Governor Len Small is second from left, future governor Louis Emmerson is sixth from the left.

Photo courtesy of the Illinois State Historical Library.

With the war's conclusion, Americans were ready for a return to normal routine, for an end to rationing and other hardships. At the election of 1920–the first opportunity for American women to vote in a presidential contest–the amiable Warren G. Harding was elected president. A genial man, Harding's election seemed to personify the national desire for quiet and "normalcy." Illinoisans elected Republican Lennington Small as governor, a staid man who had served a number of years as state treasurer.

The Small family consisted of the new first lady, Mrs. Ida Moore Small; their daughter, Mrs. A. E. Inglesh, sons Leslie and Budd, the governor's sister Sue; and Leslie's two sons, Len Junior and Burrell. Mrs. Small was characterized as "very sweet and gracious, but very retiring and of simple taste as well." She shunned publicity, telling reporters that she much preferred life on the Small farm near Kankakee. Mrs. Small had a "motherly quality" that shone through and was endearing. Newspapers remarked on the stark contrast between Mrs. Small and Mrs. Lowden, as the latter was a polished society grand dame from an immensely wealthy family who had effortlessly handled the myriad social duties of a first lady. Mrs. Small's health was not particularly good, and she in essence left many of her duties to her capable daughter, Mrs. A. E. Inglesh, who was the acknowledged "social director" of the Small administration. Mrs. Inglesh had been involved in the movement for women's suffrage, and she had traveled with her father during his successful campaign for governor.[1]

Mrs. Ida Moore Small.
*Photo courtesy of the
Illinois State Historical Library.*

Len Small was inaugurated on January 10, 1921, and that evening a public reception was held at the Executive Mansion from 7:30 to 11 p.m. In a final and touching act of service to the state of Illinois, Mrs. Lowden had decorated the Mansion with different varieties of roses, placing them in baskets and vases. The colors of the flowers corresponded to the motif of the Mansion's rooms. An estimated five thousand people passed through the reception, as Governor Small, his family, and state officials greeted them. It appears that average folks predominated early in the evening. After 10 p.m. more elite members of society predominated, as members of the exclusive Hamilton and Sangamo clubs left a party they were enjoying at the Leland Hotel and trooped over to the reception. Mrs. Small became fatigued in the course of the evening and was replaced in the receiving line by Governor Small's sister Sue. Military men, once banished by Governor Deneen, were responsible for escorting guests to the receiving line. The late war had restored the military's popularity, and its members were welcome again at Illinois inaugural ceremonies.[2]

Soon after the reception, Mrs. Small returned to the family farm in Kankakee, establishing a pattern for her short tenure as first lady. She returned to Springfield on January 19 to prepare for her first "At Home," the traditional, mid-week afternoon reception conducted by the governor's wife. The Smalls also began the typical series of dinners for members of the General Assembly. One hundred and fifty local women attended Mrs. Small's reception the afternoon of January 20, with roses and spring flowers decorating the Mansion. Mrs. Small's daughter and daughter-in-law helped insure that the event was carried off successfully.[3]

Unfortunately, such happy social occasions at the Mansion were the exceptions during the Small administration. Governor Small was indicted and tried for misuse of funds while he was state treasurer. The trial was held in Waukegan, and Mrs. Small was at her husband's side as much as her health permitted. Though Small was acquitted, he ultimately agreed to reimburse the state for hundreds of thousands of dollars. This humiliating episode and the stress of the trial harmed Mrs. Small's precarious health, fatally in the end.[4]

Mrs. Small attended the trial's closing arguments at the end of June 1922, then waited with her husband for the jury's decision. When the Smalls received the happy acquittal verdict, they began a long evening car trip from Waukegan to their farm near Kankakee. A crowd of well wishers met the Small vehicle a few miles from their home and escorted them amid honking horns and cheering. They reached home around 10 p.m. and greeted the crowd from their porch for more than ninety minutes. At 11:45 p.m. Mrs. Small turned pale and headed inside the house. "I'm so faint," she whispered to the governor, who hurried after her and caught her as she collapsed just inside the front door. Doctors were summoned and pronounced her condition grave and irreversible, the result of a stroke. She lapsed into a coma from which she never emerged. Neighbors scattered straw on the adjacent road in an affectionate effort to quiet traffic noise. Ida Moore Small died on June 25, 1922, surrounded by her family.[5]

Mrs. Small was as much celebrated for her simplicity of character, the steady, nurturing presence at home, as was Mrs. Pullman Lowden for her society polish and sparkle. She was buried on June 28 at Mount Grace Cemetery, Governor Small openly weeping as the last rites were read. Reverend George H. McClung of the First Methodist Episcopal Church of Kankakee called Mrs. Small "a queen of the home . . . a mother who lived for her husband and her children." Small received more than three thousand wire messages of condolence and twenty-five carloads of flowers.[6]

Small endured two terms as a widower governor. The death of his wife sharply curtailed the traditional social activities at the Mansion. In January 1929 another Republican, Louis L. Emmerson of Mount Vernon, succeeded Small as governor. Emmerson was another veteran office-holder–he had been Illinois secretary of state for twelve years. The new governor was a good-natured fellow, and he and his wife pledged to reinvigorate the Executive Mansion's atrophied social schedule.[7]

Entrance gates and driveway into the Mansion from Fourth Street.

Emmerson took the oath on January 14, 1929. An inaugural ball was held that evening at the state arsenal, and an estimated ten thousand enjoyed dancing and music from the Illinois Watch Band. Prior to the ball, the Emmersons held a public reception at the Executive Mansion. It was a wintry day and snow covered Fifth Street, where crowds lined up for admittance into the Emmersons' new home. The governor and Mrs. Emmerson and state officials greeted citizens in the northeast reception room, against a verdant backdrop of roses, palms, and ferns. Music enlivened the scene, with the "Emmerson Glee Club" of Chicago performing with an orchestra. Mrs. Emmerson was striking in a white velvet gown with a belt of rhinestones. She wore a diamond locket and a finger ring that were much remarked upon. [8]

The state dining room when Governor Small lived in the Mansion.

Photo courtesy of the Illinois State Historical Library.

The southwest parlor in the twenties.

Photo courtesy of the Illinois State Historical Library.

In keeping with their pledge to restore the Mansion's social life, one of Mrs. Emmerson's first acts was to hire a social secretary to help coordinate events. Miss Rena George, who had known the Emmersons from childhood, accepted the position. At the end of January, Mrs. Emmerson held her first "At Home," with some four hundred women from Springfield and throughout the state attending. A dinner for the justices of the Illinois Supreme Court followed, and the Emmersons also accepted invitations to dine at the homes of Springfield residents. The aggressive schedule of receptions and dinners was greatly pleasing to Springfield society.[9]

Mrs. Emmerson was described as a charming person who was a pleasure to know. "She has a pleasing, gracious smile, a ready wit, and a wonderful way of always looking on the bright side of life," reported the <u>Illinois State Register</u>. Mrs. Emmerson had wavy, light hair and wore rimless glasses with round lens. Her manner of assisting her harried husband was to take on the entire management of the Executive Mansion, from selecting menus and table appointments to giving instructions to the gardener. She accomplished these tasks with a boundless energy. She boasted: "I never lie down in the daytime. I do not know what it means to take a nap. My children would think I were ill if they saw me sleeping in the daytime." For Mrs. Emmerson, the Mansion was first and foremost her home, and she wanted Illinoisans to appreciate and enjoy it in the same fashion. "I love people!" she enthusiastically exclaimed.[10]

The Emmersons were blessed with two daughters, both married and living in Mount Vernon, Mrs. Harold G. Watson and Mrs. Henry B. Ward. Both daughters helped their mother with the required social duties. The Emmersons doted on their grandchildren, who often visited the Mansion, finding the spacious rooms an ideal playground. The governor always had time for his grandchildren, no matter how exhausting his day. "When he comes home in the evening, and lies down for a little rest," Mrs. Emmerson said, "the children climb all over him, and he never protests or says a word." Their granddaughter, Patricia Lou Watson, was baptized in the Mansion with Dr. John T. Thomas of the First Presbyterian Church performing the ceremony. The Emmersons held a dinner for local Presbyterian ministers after the christening. In December 1930 they hosted a tenth birthday party at the Mansion for granddaughter Widney, who invited forty giggling friends. Christmas loomed on the horizon so Widney's party adopted the season's theme. The Mansion was decked out in holly, and a giant stocking was hung from the fireplace's mantle, out of which the children each received a present. The little guests feasted on ice cream molded into candles, Santas, and reindeer, with cake and punch.[11]

The Mansion is abloom with poinsettias and decorated trees in every room at Christmas.

The state legislature appropriated $90,000 to improve and repair the Mansion. Emmerson had purportedly suggested a more modest $20,000, but a report from the state architect, who had examined the Mansion, prompted the more generous amount. Mrs. Emmerson created two sunrooms from porches on the Mansion's west side with the funds, among other more general improvements. The refurbished Mansion was ready when President Herbert Hoover and his wife arrived in Springfield on June 17, 1931.

Hoover was giving a speech at the Lincoln tomb, and he and his spouse enjoyed lunch in the Mansion's state dining room. The presidential visit was by all accounts a success.[12]

Emmerson was the oldest man at age sixty-five to become governor, and he had health problems. He declined to run for a second term. In 1932 a national Democratic landslide led by Franklin D. Roosevelt swept in Democrat Henry Horner as governor. Horner had practiced law in Cook County before being elected probate judge in 1914. Known for his honesty, Horner was a portly bachelor, and the first Jewish governor of Illinois. He was very fond of children, liked to go to the movies, and kept a picture of his mother, who died in 1921, over his bed in the Mansion.[13]

Horner's hospitality and conviviality were legendary. When the wife of the editor

The Executive Mansion in the Horner years.

Photo courtesy of the Illinois State Historical Library.

of a small newspaper in Paris, Illinois, was in Springfield for a convention, Horner made sure her visit was memorable. That the editor was a committed Republican or that he represented a small rural community did not deter the Democratic governor in the least. The wife was given a motor tour of Springfield and New Salem in the governor's car and lunch at the Executive Mansion. Such kindness prompted the Republican editor to compliment Horner for his "unquestioned integrity, ability and great personal charm." Horner genuinely enjoyed people and the myriad activities that came with his job. "I . . . marvel at your ability to enjoy anything and everything from a prize fight to a theological discussion," said Horner's friend James A. Griffin, the Roman Catholic bishop of Springfield. "You are many sided and fit nicely into any and every picture." Maybell Crawford Jones's contact with Horner at the Mansion prompted her to remark "that every moment at the Mansion House with you was a perfect delight." Horner invited James Weber Linn, a noted author and personal friend, to recuperate from an illness in the Mansion. The governor never missed an opportunity to send flowers or gifts to friends and relatives to comfort the grieving, cheer the sick or salute a happy occasion like a birthday or promotion. Such charitable acts had their political dimension, but Horner's generosity was so bountiful as to transcend the officeholder's imperative. "Money seemed to mean nothing to Horner except for the pleasure it brought to others," concluded Horner biographer Thomas B. Littlewood.[14]

A lifelong bachelor, Governor Horner was particularly fond of children. Here he savors an autograph session with a group of youthful admirers.

Photo courtesy of the Illinois State Historical Library.

Horner adored children and enjoyed introducing them to the wonders of the Executive Mansion and historic Springfield. When Rabbi Ferdinand Isserman of St. Louis wrote expressing a desire to bring his children to Springfield for a tour of the Lincoln sites, Horner quickly invited them to make the Executive Mansion their "headquarters." After visiting Springfield, a Highland Park mother thanked Horner for his overwhelming hospitality. Her boys were thrilled at the Executive Mansion and meeting the governor, and they proudly displayed the replica of Lincoln's home that Horner had given them. Little Mary Elizabeth Hughes sent a note of appreciation to the governor for her visit to the Mansion, which had included receiving a gift certain to please: "Today is the last day of Christmas vacation. I wish vacations lasted forever. School gets in my hair. I thank you for the happy days at the Mansion and also the boxes of candy. I'm taking some back to school." Horner helped with a summer camp for orphans sponsored by the Catholic Church, and he had Christmas parties for children at the Mansion. [15]

Horner had a great fondness for animals. Vaccination records for 1937 reveal that he owned six dogs: Danny Boy, a Kerry Blue terrier, Packy, a cocker spaniel, three Dalmatians, Domino, Princess, and Queen, and a feisty fox terrier named Bobby. These were prizewinning, pedigreed dogs, and they competed in shows and won awards for excellence. Their victories prompted breeders to visit the Mansion to examine the dogs as prospective mating stock. The governor helped promote the annual dog show at the Illinois State Fair, while having the good sense not to enter his own. Bobby, the fox terrier, was the governor's special favorite. "That fellow Bobby," said Horner, "has delusions of dictatorship. He wants to run everything." Bobby "patrolled" the Mansion, padding about the reception rooms, barging into the governor's office when the mood struck him, napping on the governor's bed. The little terrier liked to keep Horner company on the sofa in the reading room, gazing up affectionately as the governor perused official documents or the day's newspaper. Only Queen, who was getting on in years, and Bobby were permitted in the Mansion, the other dogs were kept in an adjacent kennel.[16]

Early in his career the governor had developed a strong and lasting interest in Abraham Lincoln. His first law partner was Frank A. Whitney, whose father, Henry Clay Whitney, had been a legal contemporary of Lincoln and had written a book on the circuit-riding era. Frank Whitney gave Lincoln books to Horner, and the future governor began to collect them. Throughout his life, Horner pursued Lincoln

An impeccably dressed Governor Horner receives an affectionate greeting from his beloved dogs.

Photo courtesy of the Illinois State Historical Library.

Governor Horner was a champion of the aviation industry. Here he peers from the cockpit of a biplane, chewing on a cigar stump.

Photo courtesy of the Illinois State Historical Library.

books and artifacts, eventually building a collection of six thousand items. Explaining Horner's affection for Abraham Lincoln, Lincoln scholar Paul Angle said Horner "derived great satisfaction from bringing himself as close as he could to a very great human being." During his tenure as governor, Horner allowed prominent Lincoln scholars to stay and work at the Mansion. Lloyd Lewis reviewed manuscripts at the Mansion. Carl Sandburg enjoyed the hospitality of the governor on a number of occasions. He borrowed freely from Horner's Lincoln library, which was located on the second floor. At his death, Horner's amazing Lincoln collection was donated, according to his wishes, to the Illinois State Historical Library.[17]

Horner kept a frenetic pace as governor in the midst of the terrible Depression. He rammed a sales tax through the state legislature to fund relief payments for the unemployed. The governor hosted a conference on drought relief for farmers at the Mansion on September 4, 1936, which President Franklin D. Roosevelt attended. The president gave a brief address from the Mansion's portico to an enthusiastic crowd, promising federal agricultural assistance. He feuded with the bosses of the Chicago and Cook County Democratic party, but won a second term in 1936. The stress of being governor when so many were suffering, the terrible workload, poor eating habits, and a sedentary life style all took their toll on his health. His papers reveal repeated illnesses that left him bedridden for days; physicians ordered him to rest in Phoenix, Arizona, in February 1934. Finally, in November 1938, Horner suffered a coronary thrombosis from which he never truly recovered. He was forced to conduct state business from his Mansion bedroom, as had William H. Bissell. An elevator was installed to save him the exertion of the stairs, and he spent months recuperating in Florida. His health shattered, Horner died on October 6, 1940, before completing his second term.[18]

Entry into gardens on the west side of the Mansion.

Horner was replaced by Lieutenant Governor John H. Stelle, who, though a fellow Democrat, was politically aligned with the machine politicians Horner detested. Stelle's brief tenure as governor, he served from October 6, 1940, to January 13, 1941, was devoted to excessive spending, awarding dubious state contracts and other questionable acts. He abused the governor's power to commute sentences, pardoning convicted criminals with such frequency that the press called him "Santa Claus Stelle."[19]

There was a palpable change in style and tone at the Executive Mansion. As one historian put it: "From a quiet bachelor's residence where Horner might discuss a Lincoln document with a friend of an evening or pore over legislative bills until late at night, the Governor's Mansion became the scene of extensive festivities, of dinners and parties." With only a short time to enjoy the perquisites and amenities of a fully staffed Executive Mansion, John Stelle seemed bent on indulging himself. He invited friends back to the Mansion in the wake of a dance at the state armory; arriving late, they roused the staff and compelled them to cook an estimated thirty pounds of hot dogs and eighteen pounds of brats. Little wonder that the Mansion staff began openly complaining

Ladies positioned the Pole Screen between them and the fire to prevent the heat from spoiling their makeup which was often wax based.

of the strange hours and constant requests for "butlering." Rumors abounded that Stelle's friends from his home region of Hamilton County were taking buses to Springfield and feasting on Mansion victuals.[20]

Still, the Stelles improved the Mansion. Wilma Wisehart Stelle, the governor's wife, determined to give the executive residence a face-lift before the governor-elect, Republican Dwight H. Green, and his wife Mabel, moved in the following January. Mrs. Stelle found the Mansion a "bachelor's shambles," with worn-out chairs, couches with stained and torn upholstery, and peeling paint on the exterior walls. The scarred brass ashtrays that the cigar-smoking Governor Horner favored were scattered about the rooms. "This is a big place and things wear out, but there is no reason it should not be clean and livable," Mrs. Stelle told a reporter. "I'm just making it presentable." Taking matters in hand, Mrs. Stelle had the house repainted and the aging furniture replaced. Only venetian blinds covered the windows – Mrs. Stelle found the draperies stashed in the Mansion's attic and had them cleaned and rehung with monk's cloth glass curtains. Horner's Lincoln library had taken up an entire room on the second floor. Mrs. Stelle had the room furnished with a beautiful French bedroom suite.[21]

Governor and Mrs. Stelle showcased the Mansion's new look at the traditional New Year's public reception on January 1, 1941, receiving guests from 2:30 to 5 p.m. Visitors gaped at the redecorated Mansion to pleasant music from the George Killius string ensemble. Ice cream and cake was served. The Stelles first and last New Year's reception marked a revival of a long tradition at the Mansion. The reception had been canceled in 1939 and 1940 because of Governor Horner's health problems.[22]

Thanks to Mrs. Stelle the Executive Mansion was in fine condition for the January 13, 1941, inauguration of Republican Dwight H. Green. A renowned former prosecutor, Green was responsible for the tax-fraud conviction of underworld kingpin Al Capone. He was a handsome man with slicked-back graying hair, who had been a college athlete and an army aviator before settling on the law as a profession. He appeared every inch a governor. He was married to Mabel Victoria Kingston, and they had two daughters, Nancy, age thirteen, and Gloria, age nine.

Mabel Kingston Green worried that the elevation of the family to the executive perch would make it difficult for her daughters to live normal lives. She tried to re-create their pleasant Chicago home life at the Executive Mansion. For example, the Greens had enjoyed grilling outdoors, so Mrs. Green had a grill installed in the Mansion's garden. She admonished the girls not to allow their new status to change their outlook.

Mrs. Mable Green
strikes a glamorous pose in 1941.

*Photo courtesy of the
Illinois State Historical Library.*

Gloria Green curls up
with a comic book in 1941.

*Photo courtesy of the
Illinois State Historical Library.*

Though they had attended private school in Chicago, Nancy and Gloria were dispatched to public schools in Springfield, a bit of leveling to offset the effects of becoming the governor's offspring.

Every first lady tries to improve the Mansion during her tenure, and Mrs. Green was no exception. The Mansion was in dire need of repair and refurbishment. The rot was pronounced–termite damage, sagging floors, cave-in of the library's ceiling. The state legislature passed a $50,000 appropriation for the Mansion. Mrs. Green immediately began a restoration effort, but with U.S. entry in the Second World War at the end of 1941, shortages frustrated progress. Still, Mrs. Green persevered. The governor's biographers described her unique skills: "She brought to this task exquisite taste, a fine feeling for harmony, and an understanding of the combination of beauty, comfort, and utility."[24]

Her handiwork in the first year of their term was revealed to the public at the New Year's open house in 1942. It was a subdued affair, coming less than a month after the terrible debacle at Pearl Harbor. The Greens felt it was better to proceed with the traditional event, as Governor Green explained later: "War is making great demands upon all of us, but in our traditions we can find the great incentive to shape our daily lives to the greatest advantage." Guests were received from 3 to 5 p.m. in the west living room. "Those who came to see what the mansion looked like after the restoration left well pleased," pronounced a columnist for the Illinois State Journal. "The interior of the old building is beautiful and is furnished in excellent taste."[25]

The advent of the Second World War brought new and unexpected challenges to Governor Green, as had the First World War for Governor Lowden. Once again the American home front united behind the young men and women on the front lines. Governor Green directed the state's war effort, and kept up a demanding schedule of personal appearances at war rallies, recruitment drives, training-camp openings, and other civic gatherings. Green and his closest advisors often closeted themselves in his Mansion office, where they could labor undisturbed. Working far into the night grappling with wartime shortages and snafus, Green would order his staff breakfast in the wee hours, and the piping hot eggs and crispy bacon would be served on a conference table amidst their work papers.[26]

The Greens tried to set an example of frugality and self-sacrifice. They organized a neighborhood scrap drive, bringing in scrap metal, newspapers, and magazines, and

using the money raised to purchase cigarettes for the troops. They cut back on their food budget at the Mansion, saving on meat and other essentials best directed to the front. Soybean loaf was served in lieu of the traditional meat loaf, a recipe that substituted soybean grits for beef. Mrs. Green emulated the example of her predecessor Mrs. Pullman Lowden and took up knitting at the local Red Cross, as well as helping at the blood bank. Daughter Nancy Green volunteered at an area hospital.[27]

Springfield was a "liberty town," a place for tired servicemen on leave to flock when released from area military bases and training camps. They streamed into town, an estimated ten thousand each month from Camp Ellis alone, a huge training camp near Table Grove in Fulton County. A massive local USO effort provided the young soldiers wholesome entertainment, nourishing meals, or simply a chance to talk with a pleasant young woman rather than a grizzled drill instructor. Governor and Mrs. Green opened the Executive Mansion to the USO and these patriotic men, staging lawn parties that featured music and dancing and delicious buffet suppers served by Mrs. Green and her comely daughters.[28]

At a USO event at the Mansion on Sunday, September 19, 1943, more than three hundred servicemen enjoyed a pleasant diversion from the war. Soldier musicians provided music, and their comrades danced in the first floor hall at the Mansion, eventually spilling out on the driveway. A buffet supper prepared by the local Daughters of the American Revolution chapter was served at 5 p.m., with seating available on

Governor Dwight H. Green enjoys a light moment with his family in 1941. From the left, Gloria, Governor Green, Mabel, and Nancy.

Photo courtesy of the Illinois State Historical Library.

In the Music room, the piano is a Steinway, and the chandelier is Baccarat.

U.S.O. Party At Executive Mansion Is Gala Event

Corporal Doesn't Recognize First Lady Of State, Finds Her Charming Dance Partner.

The local newspaper carried this story and photograph of Mrs. Green dancing with an army corporal at a USO event in 1943.

Photo courtesy of the Illinois State Historical Library.

tables placed in the garden and on the lawn. While Mrs. Green stood surveying the scene, she was approached for a dance by a young soldier. "I noticed how nice she was when I came in but I didn't recognize her," said Corporal Eli Car. "Then I asked her to dance and she said, 'Of course.'" After spinning Illinois' first lady about the room, Corporal Car came to this conclusion: "She's all right . . . She's marvelous . . . She's wonderful . . . She's charming." Mrs. Green made quite an impression as she and other USO hostesses entertained the gallant lads.[29]

After the war Mrs. Green found the Mansion increasingly lonely as the children went off to preparatory school and college, and the busy governor wolfed down his dinner before secluding himself for the evening in his Mansion office. Green's schedule made it impossible to entertain their Springfield friends, so Mrs. Green spent much time in Chicago, even after Green won a second term in 1944. The Mansion was invaluable to Green in his efforts. When a piece of legislation he favored was stalled, Green would invite groups of state legislators to the Mansion for dinner, and in the warm glow of after-dinner cigars and drinks, press them to back his proposals. Lobbying is much more likely to succeed when the recipients have full stomachs. In 1945 Green invited Chicago Mayor Edward J. Kelly, a longtime Democratic partisan, to the Executive Mansion for a conference on the city's problems. The two men agreed on an end of the ancient traction problem, leading to the creation of the Chicago Metropolitan Transit Authority. The result set the tone for constructive arrangements between Illinois' Republican governors and Chicago's Democratic mayors.[30]

Endnotes

1 <u>Illinois State Journal</u>, Jan. 10, 1921, pg. 2, c. 3-7.

2 <u>Illinois State Journal</u>, Jan. 11, 1921, pg. 8, c. 1-3.

3 <u>Illinois State Journal</u>, Jan. 19, 1921, pg. 10, c. 7, Jan. 21, 1921, pg. 12, c. 4.

4 <u>Illinois State Journal</u>, June 26, 1922, pg. 1, c. 7.

5 <u>Illinois State Journal</u>, June 26, 1922, pg. 1, c. 7-8; June 27, 1922, pg. 1, c. 5; June 29, 1922, pg. 1, c. 2. Illinois State Register, June 26, 1922, pg. 1, c. 7.

6 <u>Illinois State Journal</u>, June 29, 1922, pg. 1, c. 2, pg. 5, c. 4.

7 <u>Illinois State Journal</u>, Jan. 20, 1929, part two, pg. 4, c. 1.

8 <u>Illinois State Journal</u>, Jan. 15, 1929, pg. 1, c. 5; Jan. 15, pg. 9, c. 1.

9 <u>Illinois State Journal</u>, Jan. 20, 1929, part two, pg. 4, c. 1. <u>Illinois State Register</u>, Feb. 1, 1929, pg. 10, c. 1-2; Feb. 7, 1929, pg. 14, c. 1; Feb. 8, 1929, pg. 8, c. 2; Feb. 14, 1929, pg. 15, c. 2.

10 <u>Illinois State Journal</u>, Apr. 21, 1929, pg. 5, c. 4-7.

11 <u>Illinois State Journal</u>, Feb. 14, 1929, pg. 15, c. 4; Apr. 21, 1929, pg. 5, c. 4-7; Feb. 18, 1929, pg. 7, c. 3. <u>Illinois State Journal</u>, Dec. 14, 1930, part three, pg. 8, c. 1.

12 <u>Illinois State Journal</u>, Apr. 28, 1929, pg. 10, c. 1. Octavia Roberts Corneau, "The Governor's Mansion, 1853-1953," 161-63, Octavia Roberts Corneau Collection, ISHL.

13 Biographical statement in finding aid for Henry Horner Collection, ISHL. Thomas B. Littlewood, <u>Horner of Illinois</u> (Evanston: Northwestern University Press, 1969), 127, 146.

14 E. H. Jenison to Horner, Paris, Illinois, May 13, 1938, James A. Griffin to Horner, Springfield, Dec. 14, 1934, Horner Collection, ISHL. Maybell Crawford Jones to Horner, Wheaton, Ill., May 15, 1936, Horner to James Weber Linn, Springfield, Mar. 8, 1937, ibid. Horner's papers are replete with thank you notes for flowers and gifts. Examples include Edward Kelly to Horner, Chicago, Nov. 13, 1935, Sol Kline to Horner St. Louis, June 1, 1936, James McSherry to Horner, Springfield, Dec. 28, 1934, George Roberts to Horner, Quincy, Dec. 21, 1934, Mrs. Charles Owen Russell to Horner, Evanston, June [28], 1936, ibid. Littlewood, 133.

15 Ferdinand M. Isserman to Horner, St. Louis, MO, Mar. 15, 1938, Horner to Isserman, Springfield, IL, Mar. 18, 1938, [Lotta Ringer] to Horner, Highland Park, Ill., June 21, 1938, Mary Elizabeth Hughes to Horner, Jan. 8, 1938, Bishop James Griffin to Horner, Springfield, Aug. 11, 1938, Henry Horner Collection, ISHL. Corneau, 176.

16 Vaccination list in Henry Horner Collection, W.B. Dalton to Horner, Lawrence, Kansas, Aug. 26, 1936, quotation from <u>Chicago Daily News</u>, May 28, 1938, clipping in Horner Collection, ISHL.

17 Biographical statement in finding aid, Lloyd Lewis to Horner, Chicago, May 2, 1938, Mrs. Lloyd Lewis to Horner, [May 10, 1938]. Horner to Carl Sandburg, May 21, Sept. 2, 1936, Mar. 15, 1937, Horner Collection, ISHL. Littlewood, 24, 127-28.

18 <u>Illinois State Register</u>, Sept. 5, 1936, pg. 3, C.6-8. Horner's health problems alluded to in Horner to Edward J. Kelly, Springfield, Feb. 3, 1934, Horner to Julius Loeser, Springfield, Mar. 15, 1935, Horner to James A. Griffin, Springfield, Dec. 28, 1935, Sol [Kline] to Horner, Augusta, GA, Dec. 31, 1935, Horner to Mrs. Louis M. Katz, Springfield, Feb. 11, 1936, Griffin to Horner, Feb. 28, 1936, John Oglesby to Horner, Oglehurst, July 24, 1937, Dr. Maurice Rubel to Mrs. Cornwall, May 28, [1938], Griffin to Horner, Springfield, Apr. 8, Nov. 29, 1939, Horner Collection, ISHL. Robert P. Howard, <u>Mostly Good and Competent Men</u>, 2nd ed. (1988; Springfield: University of Illinois at Springfield, 1999), 239-45. "Horner Recovering from Severe Cold," <u>Illinois State Journal</u>, Dec. 19, 1934, pg. 4, c. 1. <u>Chicago Tribune</u>, Nov. 17, 1940, pg. 11, c. 3-4.

19 Mary Watters, <u>Illinois in the Second World War</u>, vol. 2, <u>The Production Front</u> (Springfield, 1952), 470 Howard, <u>Mostly Good</u>, 247-50.

[20] Watters, vol. 2, 470.

[21] Chicago Tribune, Nov. 17, 1940, pg. 11, c. 3-4. Watters, vol. 2, 470.

[22] Illinois State Journal, Jan. 2, 1941, pg. 3, c. 3-4.

[23] Robert J. Casey and W. A. S. Douglas, The Midwesterner: The Story of Dwight H. Green (Chicago: Wilcox & Follett Co., 1948), 222-23, 225.

[24] Casey and Douglas, 225-26. Corneau, 171-73. Illinois State Register, May 4, 1941, part two, pg. 5.

[25] Casey and Douglas, 225-26. Illinois State Journal, Jan. 1, 1942, pg. 12, c. 4-5, Jan. 2, 1942, pg. 1, bottom center, pg. 5, c. 2-3. Illinois State Journal and Register, Jan. 1, 1943, pg. 8, c. 6-7.

[26] Casey and Douglas, 254, 228-29.

[27] Casey and Douglas, 249, 252-53, 226.

[28] Mary Watters, Illinois in the Second World War, vol. 1, Operation Home Front, (Springfield, 1951), 164. Camp Ellis described in Marjorie Rich Bordner, From Cornfields to Marching Feet: Camp Ellis, Illinois (Dallas, Tex.: Curtis Media Co., 1993). Camp Ellis News, Apr. 13, 1945, pg. 12, c. 1-5, June 15, 1945, pg. 1, c. 1, July 13, 1945, pg. 4, c. 4-5, Aug. 10, 1945, pg. 5, c. 1, Aug. 24, 1945, pg. 6, c. 2, Illinois Historical Survey, University of Illinois at Urbana-Champaign.

[29] Illinois State Journal, Sept. 20, 1943, pg. 1, c. 2-5, pg. 2, c. 4.

[30] Casey and Douglas, 227, 281-82, 291.

Chapter 6

Carved marble Egyptian
lions, acquired during
James Thompson's term.

Governor Stevenson and his wife Ellen greet outgoing Governor Green and his wife Mabel.

Photo courtesy of the Illinois State Historical Library.

1949-1961: **Stevenson & Stratton,** *Patrician & Plebeian*

Governor Dwight Green hoped to win reelection to a third term, but he ran afoul of a man who would not only defeat him but go on to be the two-time Democratic presidential candidate. Adlai E. Stevenson II came from a wealthy and socially prominent family–his mother was a descendant of Jesse Fell, who had been close to Abraham Lincoln, and she owned a share of the <u>Bloomington Pantagraph</u>. Stevenson's grandfather had been vice president during the 1890s under Grover Cleveland, and his father had been secretary of state under Governor Dunne. Stevenson received an elite education at Choate, Princeton, Harvard, and Northwestern, receiving his law degree from the latter.

Governor Stevenson and his three boys next to the Mansion Christmas tree on December 28, 1949.
Left to right: Adlai III, John Fell, Governor Stevenson, and Borden.

Photo courtesy of the Illinois State Historical Library.

He had served in Franklin D. Roosevelt's administration and knew more about the federal government than state government, but Democratic power brokers wanted him to run for governor in 1948 so that charismatic University of Chicago professor Paul Douglas could run for the U.S. Senate. Stevenson agreed, though he would have preferred a Senate seat, and he bested Green in a landslide. He was married to the former Ellen Borden, and they had three boys, Adlai, Borden, and John Fell.[1]

The governor doted on his three sons, with whom he had good relationships. Like all boys, though, they tried their father's patience. After attending the inaugural ceremonies, the boys spent the night at the Mansion. Rising early, John Fell and his friend Edison Dick Jr. thought it would be amusing to ride the elevator up to the second floor and spy on the slumbering Carl Sandburg. The renowned poet and Lincoln biographer had read a poem at the preceding day's ceremonies. The mischievous boys rode the elevator up and peered into the bedroom at the sleeping poet, his white hair asunder on his pillow. When Sandburg mumbled in his sleep, the boys fled back to the elevator and in their haste pressed too many buttons, causing the elevator to jam between floors. The ensuing chaos–there was a considerable delay before the repairman arrived–made Governor Stevenson late for his first day on the job.[2]

Alas, Stevenson's inauguration as governor, a moment of triumph, was followed soon after by a personal blow–the disintegration of his marriage. The governor's wife, Ellen Borden Stevenson, came from wealth and privilege, and there were great expectations that her arrival in Springfield would herald another societal golden age of the like not seen since Mrs. Pullman Lowden graced the Mansion. Ellen's experience at the Executive Mansion was unpleasant and brief. After the inaugural, Ellen did not move into the Mansion, instead retiring to Libertyville so that youngest son John Fell could continue in school. She later acted as hostess at dinners for General Assembly members in March, but she contracted the mumps from John Fell and fled back to Libertyville. The relationship continued to deteriorate, and in September 1949, Stevenson announced the end of his marriage.[3]

Elizabeth Ives, second from left, and Governor Stevenson welcome wives of General Assembly members to a tea. After Stevenson divorced, Mrs. Ives became the Mansion hostess.

Photo courtesy of the Illinois State Historical Library.

Stevenson regarded the Mansion as a place of refuge and strength, so much so that he eschewed his State House office and conducted his affairs almost exclusively from his Mansion office on the east-side ground floor. But as his marriage disintegrated, he was desolate. "I'm alone, utterly alone, for about the first time in the Mansion," he wrote in March 1949, "gloating in self-pity, oppressed with forebodings of disaster and dishonor. Surrounded with everything for happiness and usefulness I'm desolate and destitute." His older sister, Elizabeth Stevenson Ives, called Buffie, became defacto hostess in Ellen's absence, traveling from her Bloomington home when necessary. Her husband, Ernest Ives, a former diplomat, also came to his brother-in-law's aid, at one point moving into the Mansion. The family discord disrupted the Mansion's social life in 1949.[4]

Surrounded by representatives of the dairy industry and the state Department of Agriculture, Governor Stevenson proclaims "Dairy Month" in his Mansion office. Stevenson conducted much of his gubernatorial business from his office in the Mansion.

Photo courtesy of the Illinois State Historical Library.

Buffie was naturally anxious to improve the Mansion, but the new governor kept a tight hand on expenses. When he returned from an evening walk with Buffie and Ernest to find the lights on in every Mansion room, Stevenson was enraged. "Why, the whole place is blazing! Lights on in every room–and nobody using them! I never want to see that again," fumed the governor. Stevenson religiously doused the lights as he left a room, and his relatives and staff were obliged to do the same. Buffie worried that the now ever-present darkness was attracting bats, which fluttered into the Mansion on two occasions. She tried to replace the silk coverings of chairs in the state dining room, stained from long use, but Stevenson balked at the $2,000 estimate, and Buffie had to be content with cleaning the silk and dyeing it gold to hide the more stubborn stains. The walls of bedrooms formerly occupied by Governor Green's daughters were pock-marked from school pennants stuck into the wallpaper, but again, when presented with a repair estimate, Stevenson suggested strategic placement of pictures to hide the wounds.[5]

However frugal by nature, Stevenson thought that the Mansion's walls were too bare and called for paintings and portraits to add character and color. He approached Jay Monaghan, the state historian, for assistance and Monaghan sent over a number of paintings, including a haunting Healy oil portrait of Mrs. Richard Yates that was hung in the northwest sitting room, a portrait of Shadrach Bond, Illinois' first governor, and an 1889 oil painting of Deer Park Canyon in LaSalle County by Mary Irene Barrass. The Illinois State Historical Library also sent boxes of books to fill empty shelves, including a red-bound, multi-volume collection of Civil War military records, The War of the Rebellion. The Illinois State Library contributed at least three paintings, and the Withers Public Library in Bloomington sent a portrait of Stevenson's revered grandfather who had been vice president during the Grover Cleveland administration. Governor Stevenson hung the latter in his Mansion office. He also allowed Buffie to redecorate one of the bedrooms in nineteenth-century fashion as a tribute to Stevenson's gubernatorial predecessors. Mrs. John Pickering helped with a donation of furniture that had belonged to Civil War governor Richard Yates.[6]

Governor Stevenson compares hat sizes with Gene Autry.

Photo courtesy of the Illinois State Historical Library.

Buffie worked with Helen Van Diver, the Mansion's housekeeper, or more properly house manager, who oversaw its staff of butlers, maids, and cooks. Mrs. Van Diver's husband Everett was a captain of the Illinois State Police, and he was assigned to the Mansion as chief of security. He acted as the governor's chauffeur and supervised a small security detail. The Van Divers were the only servants who lived on the grounds, in an apartment above the Mansion's garage. The cook, Gertrude "Gertie" Dent, was especially skilled in the preparation of pastries and other desserts, and she was dismayed that Governor Stevenson preferred plain fare such as applesauce, turnips, and squash. Robert Jones and Gilbert Wright were butlers, Juanita Tyler was maid, and Alberta Stovall was the laundress, along with others in similar capacities on the staff. Stevenson characterized Jones, the senior butler and valet, as "most courteous, attentive and helpful." Some of the Mansion's servants were African-Americans, and positions on the staff were much sought after in a minority community that suffered from a lack of educational and professional opportunities in the years prior to *Brown* v. *Board of Education* and later civil rights reforms.[7]

Stevenson preferred a small professional staff, declaring "I do dislike having a lot of people bustling around me all the time." Consequently, he shouldered a heavy load and put in long hours day after day in his Mansion office, causing Buffie Ives to fear for her brother's health. A familiar sight for Springfield residents passing the Mansion late in the evening was a light burning in the governor's ground-floor office. Legislative assistant Carl McGowan recalled that Stevenson "worked terrifically hard for from ten to fifteen hours a day every day!" This commendable enterprise can be partly explained as a reaction to a painful divorce. When Buffie Ives discovered her brother working in the wee hours one morning and rebuked him for overwork, he heatedly replied that having failed as a husband and father, he intended to succeed as a governor.[8]

Governor Stevenson receives some affection from his Dalmatian Artie while Adjutant General Leo M. Boyle and Mrs. Eugene Conway look on at January 1, 1953, open house.

Photo courtesy of the Illinois State Historical Library.

The Stevensons struggled with the demands of the Mansion's social schedule that first year. Of course, becoming the Mansion's defacto mistress was a great surprise to Buffie, but she took on the challenges with grace and determination, aided by her understanding husband Ernest. Traditionally, the governor hosted dinners for members of the General Assembly, justices of the Illinois Supreme Court, state officers, and members of the press. A number of local women's

Governor Stevenson hosts a dinner at the Mansion for justices of the Illinois Supreme Court. Elizabeth Ives is seated at center with her back to the camera.

*Photo courtesy of the
Illinois State Historical Library.*

French journalists interview Governor Stevenson in his Mansion office on April 5, 1951.

*Photo courtesy of the
Illinois State Historical Library.*

The women's auxiliary of the Illinois Master Plumbers Association enjoys a tea at the Executive Mansion.

*Photo courtesy of the
Illinois State Historical Library.*

organizations had been allowed to hold annual teas in the Mansion, and their officers were soon besieging the Stevenson staff for firm dates. Scheduled hours for tours had to be arranged and staff designated to act as guides. In handling these innumerable details, Buffie and other staff members relied on precedents from Green administration records.[9]

The dinners for the state legislators were duly arranged, and small groups were invited to dine over the course of the spring. The staff's inexperience was revealed when they invited members of the General Assembly's conservation committee to dinner on the same evening that the Conservation Department was holding a dinner for the same committee. Teas were also scheduled, and Mrs. Van Diver acted as the institutional memory, informing the Stevenson people that the Mansion did not host teas during the summer months and could not accommodate groups that numbered more than 350. Teas were typically held between 4:00 p.m. and 5:00 p.m. Groups that held teas at the Mansion annually included the Amateur Musical Club, American Association of University Women, and the state historical society. Sometimes, the governor would make an appearance and greet the assembled women.[10]

Typically, each governor's staff received innumerable requests for tours of the Mansion from schools and other civic organizations. It was not unusual for a group in town to view the Lincoln historical sites to end the day with a walk around the historic Executive Mansion. Each administration had to set up procedures to handle tours. Carol Evans and Margaret Munn, both Stevenson secretaries at the Mansion, were given the responsibility. At first, the Stevenson tour schedule was rather generous, tours were given Monday through Saturday from 11 a.m. to noon. Soon, the tour hours were reduced to Wednesdays from 11 a.m. to noon and Fridays from 3:00 p.m. to 5 p.m., though the staff tried to accommodate school classes that could not manage the rigid schedule. The schedule was arranged so that tours would occur when Stevenson was not in the Mansion.

He went to the State House on Wednesdays and spent weekends in Chicago. Still, if he happened to be in the Mansion, the governor might personally greet a group, though the goal of the tour schedule was to prevent his involvement.[11]

Governor Stevenson's favorite social event at the Mansion was his sister's idea. Buffie wanted to produce a history of the Executive Mansion. She envisioned inviting the daughters and granddaughters of former governors to a house party at the Mansion, which would give them an opportunity to revisit perhaps poignant memories of their years in residence. Invitations went out, and eleven daughters and one granddaughter gathered at the Mansion on Friday, June 30, and Saturday, July 1, 1950.[12]

Most of the participants had not been inside the Mansion in many years, and as they walked through its storied halls and rooms, pleasant memories came flooding back. Many were emotionally overcome. Famed historian Benjamin Thomas was on hand to record their reminiscences for posterity's sake. Florence Pullman Lowden remembered a visit by former President William Howard Taft, a rotund man who weighed more than three hundred pounds. Florence was having a party for some young friends and remembered that the ceiling shook when Taft paced around upstairs.[13]

The Stevensons threw a grand dinner for their guests on Saturday evening. Hiram Sherman, an actor and television personality, acted as master of ceremonies. Minnie Lou Giachetto sang popular songs representative

Gertie Dent, who once created "blue" food in the kitchen, with an unidentified servant.

Photo courtesy of the Illinois State Historical Library.

Honor students from Fourth Ward Chicago elementary schools were treated to lunch at the Executive Mansion.

Photo courtesy of the Illinois State Historical Library.

Governor Stevenson delivers a year-end broadcast from his Mansion office in 1949.
Photo courtesy of the Illinois State Historical Library.

of the governors' historical periods, wearing appropriate costumes. Giachetto also performed songs written by Carrie Jacobs Bond, the famous songwriter who had gotten her start thanks to the patronage of Mrs. Richard Yates.[14]

While the governors' daughters' house party did not in the end lead to a history of the Executive Mansion, as Buffie Ives had hoped, it did leave the participants with warm memories. Maurice Dunne, son of Governor Edward F. Dunne, wrote Governor Stevenson that his sister Mona was "bubbling over with enthusiasm and delight" in the wake of her visit to the Mansion. Both Eileen and Mona Dunne had returned to the house they once shared with the large Dunne brood and were very appreciative of the opportunity. The Stevensons thoughtfully allowed the Dunne girls to use their parents' old room. "I honestly believe neither of the girls had as much pleasure in many a year," Maurice reported. For quite a while after, when a visitor came to the Mansion, Governor Stevenson would urge them to find Buffie and have her describe the governors' daughters' party–evidently, it was a pleasant memory the governor wanted to share.[15]

In the days before political correctness, Governor Stevenson poses on the Mansion steps with a group of young women competing for the title of "Indian Princess" at a festival in Creve Coeur, Illinois.

Photo courtesy of the Illinois State Historical Library.

The Executive Mansion continued to be the scene of important political events. Governor Stevenson gave a deposition in the Mansion on his friend Alger Hiss, later convicted of perjury and by implication treason. An important breakfast meeting on mining reform was held at the Mansion in 1951. Stevenson was anxious to revise Illinois' aged constitution, and he endorsed a Gateway Amendment that would be a first step. It had to be voted on via popular referendum and appeared as a blue ballot. To support this effort, Buffie Ives invited twenty-three women's organizations to a "blue ballot" luncheon at the Mansion. Working with Helen Van Diver and the ingenious cook Gertie Dent, the group produced a menu of "blue" food that was colorful and delicious. Governor Stevenson got into the spirit as well, greeting the assembled ladies in a blue suit, shirt, and tie.[16]

The Stevenson boys, Adlai III, Borden, and John Fell, were scattered about at exclusive schools, but they came to the Mansion for the Christmas holidays. Borden and young Adlai slept in a room off the kitchen, while the youngest, John Fell, preferred to sleep upstairs close to his father. Stevenson and Buffie allowed the boys to host a dance party for their friends, which became quite a production. Adlai enlisted his Aunt Buffie to send invitations to friends in Lake Forest and elsewhere–in one such note, Buffie Ives characterized the event as a "genteel rout," and promised to look after the youngsters. Those coming from the Chicago area were allowed to spend the night in the Mansion. The governor and Buffie Ives were forced to surrender their bedrooms to the guests, moving into smaller rooms used by servants, while Ernest Ives acted as chaperone for those who stayed at an area hotel. The duties of chaperones in the 1950s could be onerous. As one of the dances reached the wee hours, Governor Stevenson spied a young couple in passionate embrace on the darkened Mansion staircase. He grabbed his sister by the arm and pointed. "See that. Do you think it looks safe or had you better break it up?" It seems the governor wanted the young people to have a good time, but not too good.[17]

In 1952 Stevenson found himself, despite his oft-repeated preference not to be, the presidential nominee of the Democratic party. Throughout the winter and spring, Democrats from President Harry Truman to rank and file members pressured Stevenson to run for president. He consistently demurred, firmly stating his desire to continue as governor of Illinois, though he faced a tough challenge from Republican William G. Stratton. The strain took its toll on all the Stevensons. Buffie Ives was so tense that she took up smoking, to her brother's astonishment. For her part, Buffie found the governor "obviously worried and nervous." In late July, the Democratic party met in Chicago, Stevenson was nominated, and he swallowed his reservations and personal preferences and accepted.[18]

Springfield became the headquarters of the Stevenson presidential campaign and the Executive Mansion the candidate's home base. The frenzied activity associated with the running of a national campaign swirled about Illinois' capital city. Campaign operatives rented a brick house near the Mansion and took over rooms in the Leland Hotel. The Mansion was a veritable hive of activity with press, staff, public, politicians, and photographers swarming the building and grounds. The telephones rang incessantly, and the volume of calls quickly overwhelmed the Mansion's antiquated lines. A switchboard was installed and staffed to bring order to the flood of calls. Once upon a time Governor Stevenson had answered the telephone when the staff was off for Christmas holiday–no longer! Now the governor received letters from celebrities like Marlene Dietrich and marriage proposals from eligible women interested in a stint as first lady of the United States.[19]

Fireplace from the Bartels collection.

Countless campaign events and meetings were held in the Mansion. A two-day meeting of officials of the Democratic National Committee clustered around the long conference table in the state dining room. The campaign staff came over from its nearby office for a buffet supper. Buffie Ives had a tailor come to the Mansion and fit Stevenson for a new gray suit, but the frugal Stevenson refused to part with his comfortable old shoes, which led to the most famous, and Pulitzer Prize winning, photograph of the campaign. In the end, of course, Stevenson could not overcome the immense popularity of Dwight D. Eisenhower. The governor listened to the election returns on a portable radio in his Mansion office and when the outcome was clear, calmly composed a gracious concession statement, which he delivered to supporters at the Leland Hotel. When Buffie Ives looked in on him later in his Mansion bedroom, Stevenson said he was all right, that though he had not wanted the nomination, he had nevertheless done his best and was at peace.[20]

With Stevenson's departure for the 1952 presidential contest, Democrats picked his lieutenant governor, Sherwood Dixon, to replace him as candidate for governor. With Dwight Eisenhower leading the way on the national ticket, Republican William G. Stratton defeated Dixon to win the keys to the Executive Mansion. Stratton was a youthful and tireless thirty-eight years old. He had spent much of his young life crisscrossing the state in campaigns for congressional and state offices, winning election to congressman-at-large and state treasurer. With him was his second wife, Shirley, who was a mere twenty-nine. Also moving into the Executive Mansion were Stratton's two daughters from a previous marriage, Sandra, age sixteen, and Diana, age thirteen.[21]

Governor William G. Stratton and his wife Shirley welcome visitors to the Executive Mansion.

Photo courtesy of the Illinois State Historical Library.

Shirley Stratton was young and vivacious. She had been a secretary in Chicago and was introduced to the future governor by a mutual friend. She worked on his successful 1950 campaign for state treasurer, and the two were married two days after Christmas that year. Shirley Stratton willingly embraced the peculiar rigors of political life, as Stratton's first wife had not. She embarked on putting her mark on the Mansion, making gradual improvements. She kept an aggressive schedule of tours, teas, receptions, dinners, and other social engagements. Like previous governors, the Strattons invited groups of members of the state legislature to dinner, as well as justices of the Illinois Supreme Court.

This was the 1950s, a period where millions of young couples settled in bedroom communities to raise their baby boomer children in the suburbs, linked to the workplace by a new and growing highway system. The traditional family–husband as breadwinner, wife at home with the two kids--was the norm. The governor and his wife, "Bill and Shirley" to friends, appeared to be just another young couple with children to raise, though of course life in the Executive Mansion, with twenty-eight rooms and a staff of servants, was hardly typical. But the Strattons were in many ways quintessential middle-America. Asked by a reporter what they had in store for the Executive Mansion, the Strattons said simply that they wanted to make it a good home for the girls, a "middle Illinois country house" if that was possible.[22]

Still, it was the age of Grace Kelly and Ava Gardner, one of Hollywood's last true glamour eras. Shirley Stratton was quite attractive, and she took an interest in looking her best, carefully matching her outfits to the nature of each public appearance. She had a natural poise and beauty that radiated from her, with a dazzling smile that sparkles even today from black-and-white photographs of the era. At a governors conference in San Juan Puerto Rico in 1959, pictures of Mrs. Stratton show her in a rather striking white hat, tasteful pearls, white gloves, with a large dark handbag. She looked very correct, very upper-middle class, yet her beauty was such that even in conservative attire, she had an aura of glamour. She was regarded as a great political asset to her husband, and she played a prominent role in his failed bid for a third term as governor in 1960.[23]

Shirley Stratton was very much a domestic-minded woman, despite her glamorous public image. She planned the menus each day at the Mansion, usually in consultation with Helen Van Diver, and worked with a staff of thirteen servants. The Strattons had a farm on the Sangamon River that served as a retreat for them from the demands in Springfield, and Shirley did the cooking when they spent time there. She wrote the University of Illinois for the recipe of a meat sauce she found tasty at a University-sponsored luncheon prior to the Illinois-Army game. She ordered an automatic potato peeler that promised speedy results, and she happily complied with requests for recipes to be included in cookbooks for church fundraisers.[24]

Shirley Stratton, the glamorous first lady of Illinois.

Photo courtesy of the Illinois State Historical Library.

It was important to the governor for his girls to be comfortable in the Mansion. Mrs. Stratton had three ground-floor offices, much used by Governor Stevenson and his staff, redone into sitting and recreation rooms. The two sitting rooms could be converted into bedrooms to accommodate guests. Each had distinctive themes. One was dubbed the Chinese room for its red and black color scheme that matched a Chinese painting that was a gift from the governor to his wife. The second was called the Arizona room in keeping with its western motif. The recreation room featured a ping-pong table, a game

Shirley Stratton reviews a menu in the kitchen with Helen Van Diver seated left, while Gertie Dent tends to the oven.

Photo courtesy of the Illinois State Historical Library.

A radiant Shirley Stratton poses in an evening gown.

Photo courtesy of the Illinois State Historical Library.

The Strattons celebrate Christmas in the Executive Mansion. Sandra Stratton adjusts an ornament on the tree, while Major seems interested in the large pinecone Diane is holding.

Photo courtesy of the Illinois State Historical Library.

Sandra and Diane Stratton with the family dog, Major.

Photo courtesy of the Illinois State Historical Library.

that Sandra and Diana enjoyed while listening to the latest album. It too could become a bedroom if necessary.[25]

The Strattons were blessed with many of the same group of devoted servants who had been with Governor Stevenson. Helen Van Diver continued as housekeeper, and Gertie Dent still prepared delicacies in the kitchen. Robert Jones, Gilbert Wright, and Harry O. Burns were employed as butlers, while Matilda Clanton and Lucille Tate acted as maids. Alberta Stovall labored on the laundry, and Clement Fogerty and Roy Nichols were yardmen, keeping the hedges trimmed. Many of these individuals had been at the Mansion for years, and they acted as institutional memory and support, maintaining the building and looking after the governors and their families.[26]

Mrs. Stratton allowed the Mansion to be the forum for meetings of civic organizations, and she participated in such gatherings herself. There were teas for groups such as the Springfield Woman's Club, Daughters of the American Revolution, and the King's Daughters, a women's service league. The latter organization had a "Shirley Stratton Circle," as Mrs. Stratton allowed her name to be used to promote the group. The Mansion was buzzing with activity, and visitors were pleased with Mrs. Stratton's improvements and her friendly and welcoming attitude. "Your generosity in entertaining so many groups at the Mansion has made many people happy," wrote Gladys Runkel. "I do

Governor and Shirley Stratton greet guests in a receiving line, often the opening event of an afternoon tea.

*Photo courtesy of the
Illinois State Historical Library.*

Shirley Stratton pours a cup of coffee from the silver service typically used for teas.

*Photo courtesy of the
Illinois State Historical Library.*

Governor and Mrs. Stratton, center, meet a group of foreign students.

Photo courtesy of the Illinois State Historical Library.

believe you realize what it means to us here in the community to 'at long last' have a Governor and his wife make people welcome and feel at home at your residence." The Stratton touch on the Mansion also drew plaudits. "It's perfectly beautiful, and certainly reflects your naturalness and charm!" said Mary L. Briggs. Another visitor wrote, "You've done wonders with the Mansion. I still can't believe it's the same place. You've made it into a charming, attractive home and we are all proud of you and what you've done." The tone of thank you notes to the Strattons reflected guests' feelings that they had enjoyed the hospitality of the Strattons' home, not a stuffy function at an official residence. There was a real and seemingly heartfelt emphasis on thanking the Strattons for opening their home. For example, Mary E. Broeg of Litchfield wrote: "It was so nice of you both to have so many P.T.A. people into your home to meet you and have tea–I surely <u>enjoyed it</u>." Groups that held events at the Mansion often received pictures of the occasion, a nice gesture.[27]

The Mansion was open for tours, and a variety of groups wandered about its historic rooms and hallways. Mrs. Stratton and her secretary, Wilma Shuey, conducted the tours, which were arranged by appointment, probably because fixed visiting hours were incompatible with Mrs. Stratton's busy schedule. Tours were given to every conceivable civic organization from the Girl Scouts to the Ladies' Auxiliary to the Illinois Rural Letter Carriers Association. For children and young adults, a tour of the Mansion was something very special. "I don't believe there is a single boy or girl who has ever ridden past the Governor's Mansion that doesn't sigh those 'Oh's' 'Ah's' and 'I Wonder What It's Like Inside,'" wrote Cub Scout "Den Mother" Mrs. Robert Kindred. A Mansion visit became a "treasured memory." As groups learned of the Mansion's historic legacy, the governor might emerge from his office or living quarters to greet them, quite an exciting

The Strattons partake of a family dinner in the private dining room.

Photo courtesy of the Illinois State Historical Library.

encounter for a young girl or boy. When Mrs. Agnes Anderson of Chicago brought sixty eighth graders for a Mansion tour, Governor Stratton was on hand for a hello. "It is certain that meeting the Governor and seeing the Mansion was the high point in the trip," Mrs. Anderson wrote in a thank you note to Mrs. Stratton. "It was the first thing the kids told their parents and teachers. They will never forget that day!" On the bus ride home, Mrs. Anderson overheard two students discussing their Mansion visit, concluding that Governor Stratton was a "swell guy." Mrs. Stratton received similarly good reviews. "I have never known anyone in your position to be nicer," wrote Mrs. Mabel Washbond.[28]

The Strattons lived in the Mansion for eight years, the governor served two terms, and they came to think of it as a home. They particularly enjoyed a sitting room on the second floor that had once been a screened-in porch. The Strattons could gaze from large windows at the majestic trees and greenery of the Mansion grounds, a soothing, verdant vista after grappling with the problems of state government. The governor typically relaxed here, reading a book on the sofa, and the girls labored on homework. Mrs. Stratton began each eventful day in the sitting room. She would read the newspapers, then meet with her private secretary to go over the day's schedule. Next, Helen Van Diver might wish to consult with Mrs. Stratton on menus and household concerns. Each Friday, Mrs. Stratton reviewed her annual schedule in its entirety, making whatever adjustments were necessary. Events were planned ten months to a year in advance. Whatever the demands, Shirley Stratton always handled them with dignity and grace.[29]

Entry into east gardens.

Endnotes

[1] Robert P. Howard, <u>Mostly Good and Competent Men</u>, 2nd ed. (1988; Springfield: University of Illinois at Springfield, 1999), 261-67.

[2] Kenneth S. Davis, <u>A Prophet in His Own Country: The Triumphs and Defeats of Adlai E. Stevenson</u> (Garden City, N.Y.: Doubleday & Co., 1957), 306-307, 374. Elizabeth Stevenson Ives and Hildegard Dolson, <u>My Brother</u> Adlai (New York: William Morrow and Co., 1956), 233-34.

[3] Davis, 312-13.

[4] Stevenson to Mrs. Edison Dick, Mar. 8, 1949, Walter Johnson, ed., <u>The Papers of Adlai E. Stevenson: Governor of Illinois, 1949-1953</u>, vol. 3 (Boston: Little, Brown and Co., 1973), 39. Davis, 312-13, 370. Stevenson's loneliness lingered, see Stevenson to Miss Louise Dixon, Springfield, June 21, 1951, Adlai Stevenson II Papers, ISHL.

[5] Ives, 222-223.

[6] Insurance policy on the paintings loaned by the Withers Public Library, Bloomington, and receipt to the Illinois State Museum, dated Sept. 22, 1949, Stevenson Papers, ISHL. Governor Stevenson to Trustees of Withers Library, Springfield, Feb. 16, 1949, Jay Monaghan to Mr. Ernest Ives, Illinois State Historical Library, Springfield, June 1, 1949, Jay Monaghan to Mrs. Helen Van Diver, Springfield, Feb, 2, 1949, Stevenson Papers, ISHL. Receipts from Illinois State Historical Library for books sent to the Executive Mansion, Jan. 17, 24, 31, 1949; paintings, Jan. 15, July 18, 1949, Stevenson Papers, ISHL. Davis, 372.

[7] Ives, 221, 224-25. Each day, Captain Van Diver picked up the latest newspapers at the Abraham Lincoln cigar stand and delivered them to the governor and his staff, William McCormick Blair to Captain Van Diver, Nov. 6, 1952, Stevenson Papers, ISHL. On African-Americans at the Executive Mansion see Jesse Helms to Adlai Stevenson, Committee on the Judiciary, U.S. Senate, Washington, D.C., Aug, 7, 1952, William McC. Blair to Jesse Helms, Springfield, Aug. 15, 1952, Stevenson Papers, ISHL, and Wallace Jones to Governor Stratton, Springfield, Oct. 13, 1954, Stratton Papers, ISHL.
On Robert Jones see Governor to Rt. Rev. John Chandler White, Springfield, Jan. 13, 1949 and John Chandler White to Stevenson, Springfield, Jan. 9, 1949, Stevenson Papers, ISHL. On Gilbert Wright see J. W. Mulroy to Governor Stevenson, Mar. 16, 1950, Elmer A. Suckow to Executive Mansion, Springfield, Nov. 16, 1949, Stevenson Papers, ISHL. Other Mansion staff, William McC. Blair to Mrs. Risse, Dec. 5, 1951, Stevenson Papers, ISHL.

[8] Davis, 316-17, 335.

[9] Stevenson Papers, Series IV, Drawer 8, file marked Executive Mansion Miscellaneous has invitations from Green administration events that were used as guide for Stevenson administration invitations. Ives, 216.

[10] Governor's Personal Secretary to Mrs. Meade McWilliams, Springfield, April 28, 1949, Governor's Personal Secretary to Francis G. Fernandez, Jan. 7, 1952, Stevenson Papers, ISHL. The aged Mansion was not strong enough to handle groups much beyond three hundred, James W. Mulroy to Carol Evans, Aug, 24, 1949, Stevenson Papers, ISHL. Conservation dinner conflict in R. J. Branson to Adlai Stevenson, House of Representatives, Springfield, Mar. 24, 1949, Stevenson Papers, ISHL. On teas, Personal Secretary to Miss Grace Armstrong, Springfield, Nov. 28, 1949; it appears that groups paid for associated expenses, Carol Evans to Mrs. Ives, Springfield, Mar. 6, 1952, Stevenson Papers, ISHL.

[11] Carol Evans to Mrs. Charles L. Feller, Springfield, Mar. 9, 1949, William McC. Blair to Mrs. Robert Quisenberry, Springfield, June 2, 1952, Personal Secretary to Mrs. Dickinson, Apr. 8, 1952, Blair to Honorable Robert McClory, May 14, 1952, James W. Mulroy to John D. Allen, Springfield, Apr. 6, 1951, Carol Evans to Don Hyndman, State House, Springfield, May 9, 1950, Stevenson Papers, ISHL.

[12] Ives, 239. <u>Chicago Sun-Times</u>, June 20, 1950, Stevenson Papers, ISHL.

[13] Ives, 240.

[14] Ibid.

[15] Maurice F. Dunne to Stevenson, Chicago, July 21, 1950, Stevenson Papers, ISHL. Ives, 240.

[16] Davis, 345-46, 358-59, 366-67. Ives, 221.

[17] Ives, 233-35. Adlai III to Aunt Buffie, [1949], Adlai III to Gov. Stevenson, Harvard University, Cambridge, Mass., [1949], Adlai III to Aunt Buffie, [1949], Adlai to Aunt Buffie, [1949], Stevenson Papers, ISHL.

[18] Ives, 256-257. Davis, 387-409.

[19] Ives, 255, 268, 271. Davis, 410-13.

[20] Ives, 272-73, 280. Davis, 423, 427-29.

[21] David Kenney, A Political Passage: The Career of Stratton of Illinois (Carbondale: Southern Illinois University Press, 1990), 9-10, 64-65, 71-72.

[22] Chicago Daily News, Jan. 21, 1953, pg. 18, c. 1-2, in Stratton Papers, ISHL.

[23] Kenney, 162, 169, 172, 175-76. Illinois State Journal, Aug. 3, 1959, pg. 22, c. 1-3.

[24] Majorie S. Arkwright, Food Service Manager of the Illini Union, to Mrs. Stratton, Urbana, Oct. 23, 1959, Mrs. Stratton to Mrs. Arkwright, Springfield, Oct. 30, 1959, Mrs. Stratton to the Ward phillips Company, Springfield, Apr. 29, 1958, Mrs. Stratton to Mrs. Floyd H. Whitten, Springfield, Nov. 18, 1953, Mrs. Stratton to Mrs. Merritt Wilson, Springfield, May 13, 1958, Stratton Papers, ISHL.

[25] Chicago Tribune, Dec. 13, 1953, Chicago Daily News, Apr. 15, 1953, Chicago Sun-Times, Apr. 12, 1953, Stratton Vertical File, ISHL.

[26] Employment records in Stratton Papers, ISHL.

[27] Gladys Runkel to Governor and Mrs. Stratton, Oct. 22, [1953], Mary L. Briggs to Mrs. Stratton, June 15, [1954], Harriet [Wupper] to Mrs. Stratton, Nov. 17, [1953], Mary F. Broeg to Mrs. Stratton, Litchfield, Ill., [1954], Stratton Papers, ISHL.

[28] Galesburg Register-Mail, Mar. 1, 1960, pg. 6, c. 1-3, Mrs. Robert Kindred to Mrs. Stratton, Edinburgh, Ill., Feb. 24, 1960, Mrs. Thomas C. "Agnes" Anderson to Mrs. Stratton, Chicago, May 8, 1960, Mrs. George "Mabel" Washbond to Mrs. Stratton, Springfield, Feb. 10, 1960, Stratton Papers, ISHL.

[29] The Greek Star, June 24, 1960, pg. 6, clipping in Stratton Papers, ISHL.

Chapter 7

*The fountain in the
circular north garden.*

Illinois Slum Clearance Can Start With Mansion

By CHARLES NICODEMUS
Miami Herald-Chicago Daily News Wire

SPRINGFIELD, Ill. — It's one of Illinois' most famous homes. But its bricks are crumbling and the mortar is turning to dust.

In the attic, floorboards are rotting and crack under your heel. Ceiling beams are tinder-dry. Wiring is exposed.

In the basement, ancient lead pipes are so porous they leak without cracking — then suddenly collapse.

Heavy chunks of slate from the aging roof clatter to the ground, three stories below, endangering passersby.

"It's a firetrap," confides a fireman. "I wouldn't sleep there one night."

This once-proud mansion is not in a Chicago slum clearance area, or a down-state ghost town. It's at 4th and Jackson in Springfield. It's the Illinois governor's mansion, the year-round home of the state's chief executive.

Says Mrs. Helen VanDiver, veteran housekeeper and — after Mrs. Otto Kerner — No. 2 woman in the mansion:

"The mansion is lovely to look at inside. But it's just a shell. It's a real wonder no one has been killed, or hurt, in this place."

Says Gov. Kerner: "This house is one of Illinois' most historic buildings. No one reveres it more than I do. But Mrs. Kerner and I have been

It's Worth Your Life to Live in This House

Alarming headlines prompted calls to raze the Mansion.

Photo courtesy of the Illinois State Historical Library.

128

1961-1973: Preserving the Illinois Executive Mansion

William G. Stratton hoped to win a third term as governor, but he was defeated by Democrat Otto Kerner, a Chicago attorney and judge. Kerner came from a political family. His father had a successful political career and was friendly with Chicago Mayor Anton Cermak. He sent his son to Brown University and to the Northwestern University Law School. Young Kerner practiced law in the 1930s and enlisted in the Illinois National Guard, serving honorably in the European Theater during World War II. He married Mayor Cermak's daughter, Helena, and they had two children, Tony and Helena. Robert P. Howard called Kerner "a short man with a military bearing" who was "urbane and courteous" with a "sincere manner and an ironclad memory." Kerner and his family moved into the Executive Mansion in the wake of his inauguration in January 1961.[1]

Soon after the Kerners made the Executive Mansion their home, a fire broke out in the New York governor's mansion, an aging structure, forcing Governor Nelson Rockefeller and his wife to flee. This disaster prompted press calls, some that may have been sparked by Kerner himself or his intimates, to raze the Illinois Executive Mansion and build an entirely new residence for Illinois governors. Irv Kupcinet, a columnist for the Chicago Sun-Times, suggested that the New York disaster was a graphic example of what could happen in Springfield. He called the Mansion "a decrepit, patched up building," and he claimed that Governor Kerner and his wife were worried about the potential for a catastrophe. "The mansion is a hazard, as well as horror, to its occupants," wrote Kupcinet. This grim verdict was in effect seconded by Governor Kerner. Kupcinet sent a copy of his column to the governor, who responded with an affectionate note, thanking the columnist for "the helping hand in the Mansion situation." The alarming press accounts about the Mansion's condition, portrayed as falling apart and in constant danger of bursting into flame, prompted letters from sympathetic Illinoisans urging the governor to construct a new official residence.[2]

Fears of its susceptibility to fire led the Springfield fire chief to keep the Mansion's floor plan in his car.

Photo courtesy of the Illinois State Historical Library.

Kerner asked the Springfield Department of Public Health and Safety to assess the safety of the Mansion and make recommendations. An inspection was duly undertaken and a report issued, in which it was suggested that the Mansion be equipped with a sprinkler system, additional fire extinguishers, and fireproof windows, doors, and draperies. Extension cords snaking across the rooms were removed and more outlets installed. In an extraordinary move, members of the Springfield Fire Department were required to familiarize themselves with the Mansion's floor plans, and copies of them were kept in the fire chief's car.[3]

Kerner subsequently spoke with W. J. Payes, director of the Illinois Department of Public Works and Buildings. Payes agreed that the recommendations ought to be acted upon as funds permitted and pointed out that $18,000 had been appropriated for painting the Mansion, as well as $4,850 to reinforce the floor of the music room. He suggested that Kerner draw on those accounts for repairs to comply with the recommendations. Payes argued against a sprinkler system, claiming that sprinklers only saved property not lives. Further, he pointed to a recent upbeat assessment of the Mansion's physical condition from Charles Trimble of the Division of Architecture and Engineering. Trimble wrote that the building was structurally sound, "not at all bad as has at times been reported in the press, and is not hazardous."[4]

Back in Springfield after winning re-election in 1964, Governor Kerner celebrated by cooking Lobster Almondine in the kitchen.

Photo courtesy of the Illinois Historical Library.

Trimble's assurances notwithstanding, Kerner remained uneasy about the Mansion. "If a fire gets started here, I'm afraid we won't get out," the governor told a reporter. "We worry about the kids." During a heavy rain, the roof leaked into the attic and then through the ceiling of his daughter Helena's bedroom. Mrs. Kerner solicited bids to fix the roof, but found them prohibitively expensive–she would have preferred using the funds as a down payment on a new residence, but of course that required a legislative enactment. Helen Van Diver, the housekeeper for a number of governors, described propping up the floor during dances to prevent its collapse. "The mansion is lovely to look at inside. But it's just a shell. It's a real wonder no one has been killed, or hurt, in this place," she told a reporter. Mrs. Van Diver worried that only a disaster would prompt the state to remedy the problems.[5]

Whatever his personal misgivings about the safety of the Executive Mansion, Kerner took full advantage of its historic location, four blocks from the Capitol, and beautiful interior to meet with and inspire his political allies. He had Democratic members of the state legislature over for pleasant breakfasts, which began at 8 a.m. He also employed regularly scheduled evening political meetings at the Mansion. These typically occurred at 8:30 p.m. Kerner also continued to permit local community groups to hold membership teas and other events at the Mansion. The governor enjoyed cooking, and he occasionally rolled up his sleeves and fixed himself a favorite meal in the kitchen.[6]

The negative publicity about the Mansion's shortcomings, which Governor Kerner amplified with his own complaints, prompted a movement in the state legislature to demolish the building. On June 19, 1963, the Illinois House approved a bill that appropriated $700,000 for the construction of a new Executive Mansion. The historic structure would be razed and its lot sold to developers with the proceeds earmarked to help pay for a new residence for governors. The bill's chief sponsor, Republican William J. Murphy, House majority leader, argued that the action was imperative because the present Mansion was "ready to fall down." The measure had bipartisan support–the House minority leader and whip agreed to cosponsor it. Murphy contended that after the Mansion was demolished, its lot could be sold for $750,000, which would easily finance the purchase of a new location and the construction of a new residence. The old building was a money pit that had cost the state some $37,000 in annual repairs over the proceeding twelve years. He further advocated building the new mansion in a residential area rather than downtown.[7]

Governor Kerner, far right, conducts a meeting in the Executive Mansion.

Photo courtesy of the Illinois State Historical Library.

Incredibly, Springfield mayor Nelson Howarth publicly expressed his indifference at the fate of the historic Executive Mansion, though he did hope that a new residence would be located in the city. One Springfield newspaper, the Illinois State Register, strongly supported a new mansion. The Register declared: "The present structure is a termite-ridden, weakened, unsafe, fire-trap, and should be torn down without delay." Springfield businessman Harold Prehn offered to allow Governor Kerner and his family use of the Logan-Hay mansion while a new governor's residence was constructed.[8]

The effort to demolish the Mansion caught its friends by surprise, but they were quick to marshal forces in its defense. Floyd Barringer of the Sangamon County Historical Society announced his opposition to the plan. Catherine Yates Pickering, daughter of former governor Richard Yates, Jr., sent telegrams of protest to Governor Kerner, State Senator George Drach, and even to former governor Adlai Stevenson, who was now ensconced in New York as President Kennedy's UN ambassador. "I think the great historical value of the mansion is being treated lightly by the legislature," Mrs. Pickering told the local newspaper. She speculated that someone behind the scenes was "railroading" the bill through the General Assembly. The context of Mrs. Pickerings's remarks suggests that she was referring to real-estate developers who coveted the downtown property upon which the Mansion was situated.[9]

Young guests mingle with Governor Kerner and his daughter Helena.

Photo courtesy of the Illinois State Historical Library.

Governor Kerner had never been shy about expressing his distaste for the Mansion, publicly calling it a fire hazard that threatened the safety of his family. The bipartisan House leadership may have had the governor's tacit approval in moving to do away with the Mansion. Kerner's candor made him a target of the preservationists. They peppered him with letters, telegrams, and telephone calls protesting the proposed razing of the historic building, and they also rallied their allies in the state legislature. Typical was the letter of Mrs. John Holman, who told Kerner she was disheartened "to think that the lovely mansion is to disappear from its scene." Mrs. Holman wrote a letter to the editor of the

<u>Register</u> in response to the editorial in which the paper had advocated demolishing the Executive Mansion.[10]

Bill Murphy's House measure ran into strong opposition in the Senate, perhaps a result of lobbying by preservationists. State Senator David Davis of Bloomington criticized plans to tear down the Mansion, proposing instead a study of the Mansion's problems and possible solutions. Such an investigation could determine the most appropriate answer to the ongoing dilemma–whether to raze the ancient building or preserve it. Davis believed that an honest study would conclude it was best to renovate the Mansion. Senate Republican leaders agreed. They decided to support an alternative plan in the form of a joint House-Senate resolution that called for an inquiry into the Mansion. The Murphy bill was effectively killed in the Senate Appropriations Committee.[11]

March 1965, the Illinois Division of Architecture and Engineering concluded a lengthy investigation of the Mansion's safety. Officials found that the Mansion was structurally unsound, with a sinking foundation and uneven floors. They recommended substantial repairs and characterized the building as hazardous. Buffie Ives worried that the adverse report might lead to another effort in the state legislature to raze the Mansion. She wrote to friends in Springfield and asked them to apprise her if any such bill emerged in the current session. Robert P. Howard, the <u>Chicago Tribune</u>'s Springfield correspondent, was in sympathy with Mrs. Ives's views on the Mansion, and he lobbied Kerner's press secretary, Chris Vlahoplus, for the creation of a study commission to determine what should be done with the Mansion. In response to the dire verdict of March and perhaps to the lobbying of Buffie Ives and friends, on May 20, 1965, Democratic Representative Paul F. Elward, who was the Democratic majority whip in the Illinois House, introduced a bill appropriating $1 million to rehabilitate the Mansion. Elward's plan called for the creation of a fifteen-member commission that would decide precisely how the money should be used and by whom. The commission's make-up was divided among the legislative and

Comedian Red Skelton shares a laugh with Governor and Mrs. Kerner.

Photo courtesy of the Illinois State Historical Library.

executive branches of the Illinois government–five members from the House, five from the Senate, and five from the governor.[12]

The Illinois Senate approved the House plan, though it scaled back funding to $900,000. The amended legislation was sent to Governor Kerner, who vetoed the funding while approving the creation of the commission. "I have approved the Commission because I am aware of the deep interest in the Executive Mansion on the part of many public spirited citizens who wish to preserve it for obvious historical reasons, a feeling which I share," Kerner explained in his veto message. Though anxious for the Mansion to be remodeled, Kerner had not included any funds for Mansion refurbishment in his own budget plan, and he was reluctant to accept the money provided by the state legislature. The governor had endured a spate of adverse publicity over the 1963 attempt to rehabilitate or raze the Mansion and that made him cautious where the Mansion was concerned.[13]

Elward's commission included himself as chairman, David Davis as vice chairman, Alan Dixon, Adlai Stevenson III, state historian Clyde C. Walton, and others. The commission's building subcommittee, led by Peoria architect Leslie Kenyon, produced a report cataloging the Mansion's problems and suggesting a solution. Kenyon and his subcommittee recognized the Mansion's unique character and decided it should be preserved in its glory. The verdict may well have been a recognition of the power of the preservationists, who included former governors and first ladies. As the report conceded:

Wrought iron stairway.

"Historically, the Mansion has many supporters and many people have fond memories of events in the Mansion."[14]

A number of shortcomings were described in the report. Plumbing, wiring, lighting, heating, and air conditioning were inadequate to the modern demands of a governor's residence. Personal quarters for the governor and his family, staff offices, storage space, kitchen space, all were impossibly cramped or completely lacking. The second floor was sagging to a pronounced degree, the fireplaces were unsafe, window frames were rotten, the stairs weak, and the balustrade tremulous. The roof had been repeatedly patched, the east porch was unsafe, and the front porch sagged and leaked. The location of the guard office, in a tiny space underneath the front porch, prevented the police officer from seeing people as they approached the Mansion.[15]

Kenyon proposed that three wings be added to the existing building–to the east, west, and south. Each wing would have additional space for offices, storage and living quarters. The Mansion's plumbing, wiring, lighting, air conditioning and heat plant would be modernized and brought up to code for a public facility. The roofs of the east and west wings would be terraces with Victorian gardens. The committee's cost estimate for the project was $1 million, though it recommended a total appropriation of $1.5 million, with the additional funds earmarked for carpeting and furnishings.[16]

It was soon apparent that not everyone was pleased with the conception the Executive Mansion Commission had put forward. "I am absolutely dead set against the two wings on the side of the house," declared Buffie Ives. In a lengthy letter to Clyde Walton, Ives worried that using the east and west wings as terraces would prove unsightly and impractical. The terrace gardens would be unkempt in the winter unless carefully tended. Ugly awnings would have to be employed for shade in order for the terraces to be usable in the steamy Illinois summer, destroying whatever minimal aesthetic value they possessed. Still, Ives was pleased that there was no further talk of demolishing the Mansion and that the legislature had appropriated a considerable sum for preservation. "I am very, very happy that our unusual and charming Governor's home will be preserved. It is a distinguished house, and I, for one, heard its long whispers through the night from all those who had lived there through happy and sad periods," she wrote. Walton assured Ives that the plans were merely "guidelines" subject to further discussion. Paul Elward had made a blunder when he rebuffed an early request Buffie Ives had made for a face-to-face meeting. As a result, one of the most formidable defenders of the Executive Mansion was not committed to his proposal.[17]

Plans to refurbish the Executive Mansion were put on hold when Governor Kerner accepted an appointment to the U.S. Court of Appeals from President Lyndon B. Johnson in May 1968. His lieutenant governor, Samuel H. Shapiro, filled out the remainder of Kerner's second term. Shapiro's bid to continue in the Executive Mansion was foiled by Republican Richard B. Ogilvie in the 1968 gubernatorial elections. Ogilvie had served

Governor Richard B. Ogilvie
Dorothy Ogilvie, and daughter
Elizabeth Ogilvie.

*Photo courtesy of the
Illinois State Historical Library.*

honorably as a tank commander in World War II. He was savagely wounded in the bitter fighting that presaged the conclusion of the war in Europe, spending months in the hospital. His face was permanently disfigured by shell fragments, which gave him a less than telegenic appearance just as television began dominating public life. After the war, he met Dorothy Shriver of Oak Park quite by chance while attending law school, and they married after he passed his bar exam. Ogilvie practiced law in Chicago and began to serve in increasingly important government positions. As an assistant U.S. attorney, he prosecuted organized crime figures. He was elected sheriff of Cook County in 1962 and four years later became president of the Cook County board. His successful campaign for governor followed two years later. The Ogilvies had one daughter, Elizabeth, and the family moved into the Executive Mansion on January 13, 1969.[18]

Dorothy Ogilvie inherited the problem of what to do about the Executive Mansion. Should she accept the Elward plan and its multiple wings, or could she find a solution more palatable to Buffie Ives and others worried about preserving the Mansion's unique facade? Ives had written to Mrs. Ogilvie early in 1969 to express her concerns. Mrs. Ogilvie had responded with a warm but noncommittal letter in which she pledged to maintain the character of the Mansion.[19]

Living in the Executive Mansion gave Mrs. Ogilvie firsthand experience with the foibles of the aging building. She found that the kitchen had only one sink and no automated dishwasher, though it had to handle state dinners. The heating system was terribly flawed, some rooms were hot while others were freezing. Elizabeth Ogilvie kept an electric heater in her bedroom to keep warm, a practice emulated by General William C. Westmoreland and his wife when they spent an evening in the Mansion, much to Mrs.Ogilvie's chagrin. Governor Ogilvie was often awakened in the night by the rattle of pipes. Her experiences in the Mansion convinced Mrs. Ogilvie that the building needed renovating. But she grew increasingly uncomfortable with Elward's conception, perhaps in part as a result of strong lobbying against it by Buffie Ives and others.[20]

Mrs. Ogilvie made up her mind in May 1969. She publicly attacked the plan put forward by Paul Elward and the legislative Executive Mansion Commission, staging three luncheons for journalists to air her views. Elward's east and west wings would destroy the Mansion's nineteenth-century beauty and distinctive appearance, Mrs. Ogilvie had concluded, and two trees that shielded the Mansion from nearby businesses, would have to be removed. While conceding that the demands of the modern world required expanded space for administrative and other functions, Mrs. Ogilvie forcefully argued for adding to the Mansion in a manner that would not destroy its historical appeal. That could be done with a new wing to the rear of the existing building. In response, Elward issued a rather haughty statement declaring that the final decision on the design of the Mansion restoration would be made by the commission, "not by a governor or former governor."[21]

Buffie Ives was delighted when she heard the news. "I was joyous about this," she wrote Mrs. Ogilvie, and praised her for standing up to Elward and his commission. Having taken on Elward and the Executive Mansion Commission, Mrs. Ogilvie was now faced with the unenviable task of coming up with an alternate plan for rehabilitating the creaking Mansion.[22]

Mrs. Ogilvie and the governor quickly recruited two skilled men who had just super-intended the restoration of the Old State Capitol in downtown Springfield, James T. Hickey and Lowell Anderson. Hickey was the Illinois State Historical Library's longtime curator of Lincoln Collections and Anderson was the library's historic sites curator. Hickey devised a plan to restore the Mansion and secured the services of local architects August P. Wisnosky and Carl Fisher.[23]

Wisnosky's architectural firm, Graham, O'Shea and Wisnosky, conducted its own assessment of the Executive Mansion and made recommendations for expanding and preserving it in a report dated March 25, 1970. The architects found the same problems enumerated in the 1967 study sponsored by the Executive Mansion Commission–lack of space for office, staff, and personal quarters, as well as inadequate plumbing, air, heat, and electrical systems. Overall, the Mansion was deemed structurally sound with certain exceptions, but it lacked the room required for its mission as the residence of Illinois governors.[24]

The key proposal was to expand to the rear (south) of the existing structure and keep the addition within the east-west limits of the present Mansion. As the report stated, the new addition "should not visually overpower the present structure." The ancient Mansion would be carefully preserved and remodeled under the supervision of the historical consultants, Hickey and Anderson. They would ensure that the renovation adhered as closely as possible to historical authenticity while the contractors brought the essentials–plumbing, heating, air and electricity–up to the latest standards.[25]

The new addition was a spectacular example of architectural design that combined functionality and aesthetics. Essentially, the addition provided new, roomy quarters for the governor and his family, as well as a basement and attic. The new building was physically linked to the old Mansion to give the impression of a unified whole. Storage family. The addition's first floor contained a beautiful walnut-paneled library, meeting rooms, and a public entertainment or reception area that could handle 250 people. An executive apartment–five bedrooms with private baths, a sitting room, kitchenette and family lounge, and ample storage space–occupied the second floor. The attic had a copious recreation area for children and more storage space.[26]

The existing Mansion's first floor would remain the public receiving area. Its formal reception rooms would be refinished and the state dining room expanded. The ground-floor entrance underneath the north porch would continue as the principal entryway.

The library was designed and built by Monte Holl of Decatur, Illinois, in 1971. The walnut paneling came from Illinois forests.

What had been the cramped governor's quarters on the second floor would be refurbished and converted into guest bedrooms and sitting rooms. Wisnosky proposed to reconstruct the original staircase, a bold touch. Research by Jim Hickey and Lowell Anderson revealed the elliptical shape of the stairs.[27]

The entire grounds would be relandscaped in a planned fashion to complement the historical character of the home. The old circular driveway in front of the Mansion would be demolished for a smaller, more formal terrace encircling the north fountain. The drive would be widened to accommodate parallel parking, and the north porch was expanded to allow vehicles greater room to pass underneath. A new facility would be built to the west of the addition that would serve as a more accessible guardhouse, quarters for domestics and security, and garages for vehicles.[28]

The project had a cost estimate of $1.5 million for the addition, $900,000 for the preservation of the Mansion and nearly $600,000 for landscaping, moving, and housing the first family during construction and for furnishings. Construction would begin early in 1971. The Ogilvies were moved to an apartment at nearby Lincoln Towers.[29]

The Illinois Quilt on Bartels' hand-carved bedstead took seventy-eight quilters, 4,000 hours to complete the 85"x 106", silk quilt depicting historic buildings in Illinois.

Historical accuracy was insisted upon in the renovation. "If it wasn't done right, Dick and I would have gotten the blame," recalled Dorothy Ogilvie. Historical consultants Hickey and Anderson were, in essence, leaders of the preservation effort. As work got underway in February 1971, the two historians met regularly with contractors and architects to guide the rebuilding. They handled countless questions regarding historically accurate design and construction, such as the proper shutter latches and window locks for an antebellum building. When the contractors wondered how best to relamp the cupola's chandelier, it was Hickey and Anderson who had to investigate. The two also worked closely with Mrs. Ogilvie on the selection of period furniture, furnishings, and numerous other details. Such historical minutiae required dogged research, but Hickey and Anderson met the challenge.[30]

Hickey recruited skilled millwork specialist Monte Holl to install walnut paneling and shelves in the library. Holl had worked on the restoration of the Old State Capitol. The two men had met while enjoying a musical performance at one of the supper clubs that once dotted central Illinois. Holl recalled that the work was difficult and continued after the Ogilvies moved back into the Executive Mansion in late May 1972. As he labored over the fine walnut in the library, Holl often detected the velvety odor of Governor Ogilvie's pipe. He would look up from his work and find the governor watching with a bemused expression. On one occasion, Holl smashed his finger with a hammer and let fly with a few expletives in frustration. To his horror, he heard someone chuckling and he spied Governor Ogilvie in the doorway, his distinguished visitor having overheard his angry outburst. "Watch it there, Monte," smiled Ogilvie, his face wreathed in tobacco smoke. Holl remembered both Ogilvies as considerate and deeply involved in the ongoing project.[31]

Exiled from the Governor's residence, the Ogilvies coped as best they could. They conducted their social dinners and receptions at alternate locations. When Congressman Wayne N. Aspinall visited Springfield, governor and Mrs. Ogilvie held a reception in his honor at the Old State Capitol. Invitations contained an explanation for the change of venue: "The Executive Mansion . . . is presently undergoing a long overdue and extensive renovation." Special parking arrangements were made for the guests. Tours of the Mansion, which was in every respect a construction site, continued during the renovation, at least for select groups. Hickey and Anderson handled the tour arrangements, selecting a safe, as well as informative, route amidst the laborers and the detritus of a construction zone.[32]

State funds covered both the new addition and the necessary structural repairs to make the old Mansion safe. Furniture and various furnishings in the quarters were also provided by state appropriations. (Governors could also bring their own furniture and comforts.) The public rooms in the historic Mansion needed to be furnished with period antiques and objects that matched and complemented the venue and its mission.[33]

To provide these antiques and other treasures, the Illinois Executive Mansion Association (IEMA) was created, a nonprofit corporation that solicits tax deductible contributions to furnish the public rooms of the Illinois Executive Mansion. The organization was modeled after the successful White House Association, which fulfilled a similar purpose for the president's famous residence. The mission of the IEMA is ongoing, and the current first lady, Lura Lynn Ryan, is honorary chairwoman. The first president of the IEMA, Margaret Van Meter, was joined by Hope McCormick as vice president, Devera Victor as secretary, James T. Hickey as treasurer, and Ralph G. Newman as trustee. Van Meter and the other officers got the association underway and raised thousands of dollars for priceless period furniture, paintings, and other beautiful objects that enhance the majesty of the Executive Mansion.[34]

Hand-carved sofa from the Bartels collection.

Ogilvie faced the formidable campaigning talents of Democrat Dan Walker in the 1972 election. The governor hoped to disprove his buttoned-down, stoic image, a drawback in the psychedelic 70's. "It is unavoidable that, when you're governor, you get an aloof reputation," declared Ogilvie, who had, after all, served as an enlisted man and tank commander in the army, hardly a sign of elitism. "You just can't talk to everybody if you're going to be a good governor. But, I can have fun too, and match Walker stride for stride." To prove he was one of the boys, Ogilvie walked into a Pittsfield tavern while on a campaign tour, bought a round for the house, and then challenged and defeated some of the locals at shuffleboard. In the end, an unbuttoned Ogilvie could not overcome the campaign gimmickry of Dan Walker, nor appease those who blamed him for the state income tax, Paul Powell, and racetrack corruption. Though personally above reproach, Ogilvie was a convenient target, and he went down to defeat.[35]

The Ogilvies soothed their wounded pride with a pleasant New Year's Eve celebration at the Mansion with good friends, including Margaret Van Meter who had done so much in the effort to provide furnishings for the historic residence. They gathered at the piano and sang old favorites together, laughing while reflecting on bittersweet memories and years. Adjourning to the Mansion's new private quarters, the governor and the other husbands enjoyed cards until the New Year dawned. Then they kissed their wives and raised their glasses to toast. The Ogilvies actual time in residence at the Mansion had been brief, but they had shepherded the preservation of a priceless repository of Illinois history.[36]

East gardens with trellis.

Endnotes

[1] Kerner biography in Otto Kerner Papers, ISHL. Robert P. Howard, <u>Mostly Good and Competent Men</u>, 2nd ed. (1988; Springfield: University of Illinois at Springfield, 1999), 280-281.

[2] The fire at the New York governor's mansion in Albany on March 3, 1961, revealed that Nelson Rockefeller and first wife Mary Todhunter Clark were having marital problems. Newspaper reporters noted that firemen rescued Mrs. Rockefeller from a separate Mansion wing from the location of her hus band's bedroom. The Rockefellers were later divorced, and Governor Rockefeller purportedly had his first wife's name expunged from a history of the New York governor's mansion. Peter Collier and David Horowitz, <u>The Rockefellers: An American Dynasty</u> (New York: Holt, Rinehart and Winston, 1976), 346-48. <u>Chicago Sun-Times</u>, Mar. 5, 1961, Kupcinet to Kerner, Chicago, Mar. 4, 1961, Kerner to Kupcinet, Mar. 17, 1961, <u>Miami Herald</u>, Aug. 6, 1961, Mrs. Violet Carrol to Kerner, Oak Lawn, Ill., Mar. 22, 1961, Kerner to Mrs. Carrol, Springfield, Mar. 28, 1961, Kerner Papers, ISHL.

[3] Frederic S. O'Hara to Governor and Mrs. Kerner, Department of Public Health and Safety, Springfield, Mar. 20, 1961, Kerner Papers, ISHL.

[4] Payes to Otto Kerner, Dept of Public Works and Buildings, Springfield, Mar. 28, 1961, Charles Trimble to R. D. Henderson, Division of Architecture and Engineering, Springfield, Mar. 23, 1961, Kerner Papers, ISHL.

[5] <u>Miami Herald</u>, Aug. 6, 1961, in Kerner Papers, ISHL.

[6] Kerner to Anthony Scariano, Park Forest, Ill., Springfield, Mar. 15, 1961, Kerner to James W. Gray, Apr. 7, 1961, Kerner Papers, ISHL. <u>Illinois State Register</u>, June 16, 1963, pg. 25, c. 2-3. <u>Illinois State Register</u>, May 20, 1978, Illinois Executive Mansion Restoration, ISHL.

[7] <u>Illinois State Journal</u>, June 20, 1963, pg. 1, c.5-7, pg. 2, c.2, June 29, 1963, pg. 1, c. 4-5.

[8] <u>Illinois State Journal</u>, June 20, 1963, pg. 2, c. 2. <u>Illinois State Register</u>, June 17, 1963, pg. 6, c. 1-2, June 20, 1963, pg. 1, c. 1-4.

[9] Floyd S. Barringer to Otto Kerner, Springfield, July 1, 1963, Kerner Papers, ISHL. <u>Illinois State Journal</u>, June 20, 1963, pg. 50, c. 1-3. Catherine Yates Pickering to Governor Kerner, telegram, June 20, 1963, Kerner Papers, ISHL.

[10] Mrs. John Holman to Governor Kerner, Springfield, June 17, 1963, Kerner Papers, ISHL. See also Richard C. Thorpe to Mrs. Winifred Barringer, June 20, 1963, Thorpe to Mrs. Catherine Pickering, June 20, 1963, Thorpe to Miss Irene Garvey, June 21, 1963, Kerner Papers, ISHL.

[11] <u>Illinois State Journal</u>, June 22, 1963, pg. 1, c. 1-2, June 26, 1963, pg. 11, c. 1-2.

[12] <u>Illinois State Journal</u>, May 21, 1965, Robert P. Howard to Mrs. Ives, Springfield, May 6, 1965, Jo Saner to Mrs. Ives, Springfield, May 12, 1965 in Ives Papers, ISHL.

[13] <u>Report to Illinois General Assembly by the Executive Mansion Commission with Recommendations for Action</u>, March, 1967, Robert P. Howard to Mrs. Ives, Springfield, May 6, 1965, Ives Papers, ISHL. Kerner veto message in Illinois Executive Mansion Restoration, ISHL.

[14] <u>Report to the Illinois General Assembly by the Executive Mansion Commission with Recommendations for Action</u>, March 1967, Ives Papers, ISHL.

[15] Ibid.

[16] Ibid.

[17] Mrs. Ives to Mrs. Walter P. Paepcke, Oct. 23, 1967, Mrs. Ives to Clyde C. Walton, June 13, 1967, Clyde C. Walton to Mrs. Ives, Dekalb, IL, Oct. 14, 1968, Ives Papers, ISHL.

[18] Howard, 293-95. Taylor Pensoneau, <u>Governor Richard Ogilvie: In the Interest of the State</u> (Carbondale: Southern Illinois University Press, 1997), 1-4, 228-29.

[19] Dorothy Ogilvie to Mrs. Ives, Springfield, Feb. 19, 1969, Ives Papers, ISHL.

[20] "Governor's Wife Queries Repairs," unsigned Associated Press report, [May, 1969], unknown newspaper, Ives Papers, ISHL.

[21] Buffie Ives to Mrs. Richard B. Ogilvie, May 10, 1969, Ives Papers, ISHL.

[22] Unknown newspaper clipping, Chicago Sun-Times, Dec. 21, 1969, Illinois Executive Mansion Restoration, ISHL.

[23] Pensoneau, 230-31.

[24] Graham, O'Shea and Wisnosky, "The Executive Mansion: A Program for Preservation and Expansion," Mar. 25, 1970, Illinois Executive Mansion Restoration, ISHL.

[25] Ibid.

[26] Ibid.

[27] Ibid. News release, Feb. 11, 1971, Governor's Mansion, Verticle File, ISHL.

[28] Invitation to Aspinall reception, meeting and meeting minutes, Mar. 22, 1972, Illinois Executive Mansion Restoration, ISHL.

[29] Ibid.

[30] Pensoneau, 230. "Houseful of History: The Executive Mansion," Dispatch (June, 1972). A&P Meeting Minutes, May 31, 1972, June 26, 1972, Sep. 7, 1971, Illinois Executive Mansion Restoration, ISHL.

[31] Pensoneau, 251.

[32] "Graham, O'Shea and Wisnosky, "The Executive Mansion: A Program for Preservation and Expansion," Mar. 25, 1970, Illinois Executive Mansion Restoration, ISHL.

[33] Monte Holl, interview with author, Decatur, IL, Sep. 2000.

[34] Unsigned notes on the raison d'être of the Illinois Executive Mansion Association, Ralph G. Newman to Mrs. Ogilvie, Springfield, Feb. 28, 1972, Newman to Sheldon S. Cohen, IEMA, Springfield, Apr. 14, 1972, Remarks of Margaret Van Meter, undated, Illinois Executive Mansion Restoration, ISHL.

[35] Pensoneau, 269.

[36] IEMA memo, undated, Illinois Executive Mansion

Chapter 8

Side view of the west side of Mansion. This extension was added in 1972.

Governor Daniel Walker and his wife Roberta Walker.

Photo courtesy of the Illinois State Historical Library.

1973 –1999: A New Executive Mansion

Daniel Walker's dramatic walk-across-the-state campaign had propelled him into the governor's office. The typically gracious Ogilvies invited the incoming governor and his wife Roberta for lunch at the Mansion on January 3, 1973, giving them a look at their newly renovated home. The following week, on Tuesday, January 9, 1973, Walker was sworn in on the Capitol grounds in freezing temperatures. After the inaugural ceremony, 425 persons enjoyed a luncheon at the Mansion, a demonstration of its greater capacity and functionality. Guests strolled about the carpeted public rooms, sipped champagne, and gazed at the barren splendor—some of the rooms still lacked the requisite furniture. The visitors were shepherded into the new south meeting room, where lunch was served on tables sporting yellow linen with matching napkins, a bottle of rosé wine, and an arrangement of fresh flowers. They partook of a sumptuous repast of standing rib roast, roasted Cornish hen, and various finger foods.[1]

Governor Walker amuses his son Billy on the Mansion lawn.

Photo courtesy of the Illinois State Historical Library.

Daniel and Roberta Walker enjoyed the blessings of the largest gubernatorial family since the Dunnes: Kathleen, 24, Dan Jr., 23, Julie Ann, 22, Roberta Sue, 20, Charles, 18, Margaret Ann, 13, and Billy, 10. The younger children attended Holy Cross school in Deerfield where they resided prior to their move to the Mansion. Mrs. Walker wanted the children to finish out the term at Holy Cross before transferring to a Springfield school. With an abundance of children come pets. Unlike their dog-loving predecessors, the Walkers liked cats; they had three—Tiger, Kitty Gray, and Mergie. A white mouse and various species of fish and turtle completed the menagerie.[2]

Soon after the Walkers moved into the Mansion, their eldest daughter Kathy married David Hall Vaught at St. Joseph Catholic Church in Chatham on January 20, 1973. The newlyweds met while volunteering on the bride's father's campaign for governor. The wedding mass occurred at 2 p.m., and the Walkers held a reception at 4 p.m. at the Mansion. Simplicity was the hallmark of the wedding–the Chatham church was small, and the Mansion was reportedly unadorned with the usual garlands typical of a wedding reception. Champagne was provided to accompany food and pleasant music. In April, Julie married James A. Kollar and another Mansion reception followed.[3]

Illinois Executive Mansion Association co-chairman Margaret Van Meter welcomed the Walkers to Springfield and informed Mrs. Walker that as first lady she was honorary chairman of the IEMA. Mrs. Walker willingly embraced the relentless fund-raising demands necessary to complete the furnishing of the Mansion. Jim Hickey and Lowell Anderson continued to purchase furniture at New Orleans specialty shops, engaging in a Herculean effort to bring beautiful pieces to the Mansion. It is impossible to credit them enough for the ultimate success of the endeavor. The IEMA constantly raised money as it emptied its coffers to buy more furniture, then refilled them and repeated the process.[4]

Various projects were launched to generate the necessary funds. For example, groups in Illinois cities gathered donations to furnish a particular room. Mrs. Hilliard Shair of Quincy led a successful effort in that city to furnish the northwest sitting room, raising $8,000. A similar group in Kankakee was also working to furnish the Mansion. Mrs. Walter J. Charlton led the fundraising drive, convincing some seventy women to donate $100 each, in exchange for which they were treated to lunch at the Mansion with Mrs. Walker. The contributors included members of the families of former governors Len Small and Sam Shapiro. The $7,000 raised was earmarked for scenic wallpaper for the "Kankakee Room." The wallpaper detailed picturesque scenes from antebellum New York City, West Point, Boston, Niagara Falls, and the Natural Bridge. Springfield too helped with two benefits. The first was a performance of the National Academy Arts Ballet at Springfield High School on December 14, 1974. Judy Bartholf and Barbara Stackler handled the arrangements, which included a Mansion buffet hosted by the Walkers after the show. The program generated $9,000. The following year, the Chicago Symphony Orchestra performed in Springfield at the behest of the Mansion Association.[5]

The National Academy Ballet performed at Springfield High School in a 1974 benefit for the Mansion.

Photo courtesy of the Illinois State Historical Library.

Governor and Mrs. Daniel Walker
and
The Illinois Executive Mansion Association
cordially invite you to attend
a
Holiday Performance
of the
National Academy Ballet
to benefit the
Mansion Restoration Project

Buffet Reception
immediately following the Ballet
Executive Mansion

December 14th, 1974   Curtain: 8 o'clock
Springfield High School   Black Tie

The IEMA also staged a benefit performance in Chicago by famed opera diva Maria Callas, her first performance in the Windy City in sixteen years. Callas's voice range had declined with age, and a bad cold hampered the performance of her accompanying tenor Giuseppe di Stefano. Critics found plenty of which to be critical, but the concert gathered in some $60,000 to furnish the Mansion. The project was the result of the hard work of Tish Hewitt, Geraldine Freund, and Bonnie Swearingen. After the show, a dinner was held at the Drake Hotel, where Callas was staying. The star was supposed to appear and mingle at the dinner, but, true to diva form, she remained closeted in her room with a few old Chicago-area friends. Governor Walker and Mrs. Walker, former governors Ogilvie and Stratton, and their wives attended the performance.[6]

Many individuals and civic organizations contributed cash or donated furniture, paintings, and other objects to furnish the Mansion. The Illinois Federated Women's Club helped purchase candle girandoles and a teak stand. Mrs. Christina Jones, who represented the Miss Eliza Condell estate, donated eighteen prints that were hung in pairs about the Mansion. A painting of historic Camp Butler was transferred from the Camp Lincoln National Guard warehouse, and Mrs. Robert Mayer donated an oriental vase. Field Enterprises contributed to furnish one of the parlors, while Ben and Devera Victor gave both money and English prints. Mrs. Thomas A. Scully took charge of raising the necessary funds to landscape the grounds, staging a benefit garden party at her home.[7]

Jim Hickey, as always, went beyond the ordinary in his generosity. In addition to donating his own money, he led successful efforts to acquire furnishings. He contacted Robert Todd Lincoln Beckwith, who agreed to donate china, an inlaid table, and a portrait of Mrs. Lincoln. Hickey also obtained framed documents that featured the signatures of former governors of Illinois. The official papers hang today in an east-west corridor in the Mansion.[8]

An invitation to the Maria Callas benefit concert.

Photo courtesy of the Illinois State Historical Library.

Perhaps the most dramatic acquisition of the Walker era came from John M. Olin, who in 1975 donated his $3 million estate to the Southern Illinois University at Edwardsville. Olin's mansion at Fairmont, near Alton, contained numerous items of antique furniture, china, and other objects. Impressive paintings came to the Mansion from the Olin estate, including Francisco Goya's portrait of Ferdinand VII, a Gilbert Stuart portrait of Meriwether Lewis, and three works by George Romney. Margaret Van Meter, whose husband was a member of the university's board, approached the university about the possibility of loaning the Olin property to furnish the Executive Mansion. The university agreed. "It is believed that these valuable and largely irreplaceable articles will serve a higher public purpose at the Executive Mansion than would be served by them in the context of the University's use of the Olin property as a cultural and conference retreat center," declared SIU-E Acting

The Fine Arts Committee
under the Sponsorship of the
Illinois Executive Mansion Association
invites your participation
to assist in the Fund Raising Benefit
for the
Executive Mansion Association
by attending the only performance of
Maria Callas
and a
Gala Ball
following the concert
on Saturday, the second of March
on the Stage of the Opera House
20 North Wacker Drive
Chicago, Illinois

White or black tie   Curtain: 8:00 o'clock

Governor James R. Thompson.
Photo courtesy of the Illinois State Historical Library.

President Andrew J. Kochman. Value of the numerous items was variously estimated in news accounts at from $250,000-$500,000. Mrs. Walker, Margaret C. Dowling, and Jim Hickey traveled to the Olin property and selected the items for transfer to the Mansion.[9]

In 1976 Daniel Walker was defeated in the Democratic primary for a second term as governor by Michael J. Howlett, who was the secretary of state. Howlett faced a formidable Republican in the 1976 general election for governor. James R. Thompson had been an U.S. Attorney for the Northern District of Illinois, successfully prosecuting a number of high officials for corruption, including, sadly, former governor Otto Kerner. In the Watergate era, with great public concern over corruption and record crime rates, Thompson personified the antidote–a crime-fighting, corruption-busting prosecutor. He defeated Howlett and continued as governor for fourteen years, serving four terms.[10]

Governor Thompson was married to Jayne Carr Thompson, a native of Oak Park and a lawyer and prosecutor in her own right. She was employed in the Illinois Attorney General's office, but resigned after her husband became governor. Like her predecessors as first lady, she became honorary president of the IEMA, and she embraced the Mansion and her role as manager. "The mansion doesn't really belong to us, it belongs to the people," she affirmed with plebeian emphasis. Her first days in the Mansion, she recalled with a laugh, were spent simply finding her way about the cavernous interior. "The ground floor I found confusing because the hallway looked exactly the same at both ends . . . I'd get off the elevator and I'd be going to this sitting room and I'd end up in the governor's office," she remembered.[11]

The Thompsons coped with the demands of their schedules by maintaining a sense of humor and enjoying leisure time with each other. "One of our favorite nights is when I fix dinner and we just sit around and read and relax. It's a pleasure for us not to have anything we HAVE to do in 20 minutes," she said. The governor was especially fond of the beautiful walnut-paneled library and, if he came home early, liked nothing better than to build a warm fire in the fireplace and stretch out. One of their most pleasant pastimes was antiquing, exploring antique shops and auctions for bargains and overlooked treasures. Indeed, Governor Thompson and his wife had a passion for antiques and artwork, and they eagerly took on the continuing task of decorating the Mansion.[12]

The Thompsons endured a spate of bad publicity as they took advantage of the new, more commodious Mansion to entertain. In the election year of 1978, food and beverage expenses at the Mansion were made public, prompting criticism for supposed high living on the taxpayer. Bills for $1,550 for seafood such as lobster tails and shrimp drew cries of "Camelot has come to the cornfields." In truth, the governor was simply using the Mansion as it had always been intended–for dinners, luncheons, receptions, and meetings related to the business of the State of Illinois. With roomier facilities, thanks to the Ogilvie restoration, larger groups could be accommodated, and with the greater crowd came bigger bills. Mrs. Thompson defended her handling of the Mansion. "Most people can't identify with a 40-room house and understand the special problems," she said. "The people of the state paid $3 million to restore this mansion, and I feel we owe them an obligation to keep it in decent shape." The feisty Thompson released a detailed refutation, comparing his bills to Governor Walker's and concluding the he (Thompson) had reduced expenditures.[13]

While the magnificent Olin donation had largely completed the furnishing of the Mansion, some rooms still lacked particular pieces. Governor and Mrs. Thompson willingly shouldered fundraising duties for the IEMA, and because of their shared passion for antiques and art, relished the task of scouring the art world for unique objects and furniture for the Mansion. Exciting fundraising events were the norm during the Thompson era. The proceeds of a $100 per ticket performance by Liza Minelli in *Shine It On* at the Shubert Theatre in Chicago went to the Mansion. Jayne Thompson and Bonnie Swearingen co-chaired a showing of the summer fashions of designer Oscar de la Renta at Zorines in Chicago, again to benefit the Mansion. At the April 26, 1978, Chicago Antique Show, the organizer agreed to allow a private showing prior to the official opening with proceeds for the IEMA. There were annual balls, Christmas events, and Indian Summer Antique Fairs—all to raise money for IEMA. Following the lead of Quincy, Kankakee and other cities, a group formed in Rockford to raise money to furnish a second-floor sitting room, dubbed the Rock River Valley Room. Mrs. Albert K. Madlener, Jr., daughter of Governor Frank Lowden, was honorary chairman of the Rock River group.[14]

Invitation to the Oscar de la Renta Spring Collection benefit.

Photo courtesy of the Illinois State Historical Library.

And Governor and Mrs. James R. Thompson

cordially invite you to join them on

Wednesday, February 22, 1978

for the special presentation by

I. Magnin

of the

Oscar de la Renta Spring Collection

Zorine's
One West Maple Street
Chicago, Illinois

R.S.V.P. by
February 15, 1978

6:30 p.m. Cocktails
7:15 p.m. Fashion Show
Buffet supper immediately
following the show

The money raised was used to retire existing debt and to acquire additional furniture and art. The governor also remodeled the family quarters during his tenure. Much of the art was discovered and selected by Governor and Mrs. Thompson. Among the paintings acquired during the Thompson administration were John Worf's watercolor *Abraham Lincoln's Cottage*, Allen Tucker's *Summer Hillside*, and Harriet R. Lumis's *At the Wharf*. Governor Thompson's most notable acquisition was a suite of furniture carved in the nineteenth century by Carthage farmer William J. Bartels. Born in Germany, Bartels emigrated to the United States where he farmed for a time before indulging his passion for woodcarving. He created furniture from white oak and birch with elaborate and intricate ornamentation that imitated Illinois flora such as wild roses, ferns, and white oak leaves. Bartels's collection had been displayed at the 1893 Columbia Exposition in Chicago at the behest of Illinois governor John P. Altgeld. In 1980, Governor Thompson learned that Bartels's work was to be sold at auction in New York. He raised $45,000 and dispatched Springfield resident Frank Mason to bid on the collection. Mason purchased the Bartels furniture for $38,885, a bargain price. On December 20, 1980, Governor Thompson hosted a tour of the new Bartels bedroom and sitting room, which he named the John P. Altgeld suite, with a lovely dinner afterwards for the donors who had made the purchase possible.[15]

In remembrance of American hostages in Iran, Jayne Thompson ties a yellow ribbon around a tree on the Mansion grounds.

Photo courtesy of The State Journal-Register.

The Thompson family participates in a Christmas tree lighting ceremony at the Mansion.

Photo courtesy of The State Journal-Register.

On Christmas morning 1977, Jayne Thompson gave her husband most welcome news: she was pregnant. The following year, on August 3, 1978, Samantha Jayne Thompson was delivered at Springfield's Memorial Medical Center. She was the first baby born to an Illinois gubernatorial family since the Deneens early in the century. The governor and Mrs. Thompson were naturally thrilled. They had decorated a nursery in the Mansion with antiques and loads of stuffed animals the governor had acquired on his travels to state and county fairs.[16]

For the first five years of her life, Samantha grew up in the fishbowl existence of the Executive Mansion. A doting Mansion staff surrounded and petted her, and when she went out, a state trooper dogged her heels. She has many fond memories of those years. "I remember running up and down the hallway of the (mansion's) family quarters," she recalled. "I remember sitting in my parents' bed on Sunday while they read the paper. I used to get up every morning at the crack of dawn. I'd go downstairs and get dressed in the locker room where people who worked at the mansion changed their clothes. Then I'd go bother the secretaries for a little while. Then I would slide down some banisters or go up and play Pac-Man in the attic. I was all over the place. I was supervised by everybody. Whoever saw me would take care of me." Her parents worried that this peculiar lifestyle was detrimental, and when Samantha was five, they moved her to Chicago. "I want[ed] her to have a chance in life to just be a kid for a while," the governor explained. "That's why we moved out of the mansion. She was getting to an age where she was becoming too impressed by a mansion with a butler and 42 rooms. That's not

Governor Thompson and wife Jayne bring baby Samantha home to the Mansion.

Photo courtesy of
The State Journal-Register.

Governor and Mrs. James R. Thompson
invite you to the
Exclusive Preview Showing
for the benefit of the restoration of
The Governor's Mansion
of the State of Illinois

FIRST CHICAGO ANTIQUE SHOW

The Expo Center of the Apparel Mart
350 North Orleans Street   Chicago, Illinois

Wednesday, April 26, 1978 $50.00 Contribution
7:00 — 10:00 p.m.   Tax Deductible

**This ticket may also be used for
free admission to the show at any time**

Make check payable to: Illinois Executive Mansion Association

Invitation to fundraising event
for the Mansion.

*Photo courtesy of the
Illinois State Historical Library.*

Samantha Thompson gives her father a hug at an antique fair.   *Photo courtesy of The State Journal-Register.*

the way her mother and I have raised her." Samantha attended Chicago area schools and then Georgetown University. She has, by all accounts, grown into a confident young woman with a bright future.[17]

Governor Jim Thompson's long and unprecedented run as Illinois' chief executive came to a close in 1991 with the inauguration of Republican Jim Edgar, who had defeated Democrat Neil Hartigan the previous year. Edgar was a native of Charleston with a compelling personal history. The youngest of three children, Edgar was seven-years-old when his father Cecil was killed in an automobile accident. His mother Betty Edgar learned to type and worked to support her three children, eventually landing a job at Eastern Illinois University. She refused to sue the truck driver who was involved in the accident that led to her husband's death, and she would not go on disability when she was unemployed. Jim Edgar grew up in a household that was necessarily frugal, with a mother who was the living embodiment of courage, self-sacrifice, and hard work. He attended Eastern Illinois University, and

Dakota Edgar gives the governor a bit of assistance with the media swarm.

Photo courtesy of Governor and Mrs. Edgar.

as he matured, he demonstrated those same values. He was a serious man, not dour, but sober and responsible. As a student, he was a devout Baptist in the 1960s, a time when many chose to jettison traditional mores. Edgar held to his principles. He met Brenda Smith while at Eastern–she was from Anna in southern Illinois–and they married. They have two children, Brad and Elizabeth.[18]

The Edgar years in the Mansion reflected those same Midwestern values. Mrs. Edgar tackled an aggressive agenda of issues devoted to women and children. Though by nature "a private and reserved person," Mrs. Edgar overcame her reticence and plunged into the role of first lady. She acted as spokesperson and guiding light of the Help Me Grow campaign, an effort to increase public awareness of programs that

Mrs. Edgar holds a
P.J. Huggabee teddy bear.

*Photo courtesy of
Governor and Mrs. Edgar.*

helped parents and children by providing child safety seats, immunizations, and nutrition education, among many other things. With the cooperation of Marshall Field's department store, the P.J. Huggabee teddy bear was distributed to foster children who had been abused. In the wake of the Oklahoma City bombing, Mrs. Edgar dispatched 30,000 teddy bears to the families and children who had been afflicted in that tragedy. She traveled around the state promoting immunization, and in 1997 she held a conference on preventing youth violence at the Mansion. She tirelessly promoted mammograms for women and worked to streamline the adoption process so children could be placed with loving parents. Mrs. Edgar's two terms as first lady were certainly active and productive.[19]

Though quite busy with those policy priorities, Mrs. Edgar did not neglect the traditional duty of a first lady to manage the Mansion. "We are living in a house that belongs to the people of Illinois," she said. "I feel responsible for preserving this historic residence." She worked closely with the Illinois Executive Mansion Association to ensure the success of the continued fundraising necessary for the upkeep of the public rooms. She found deteriorating drapes and threadbare carpet that caused people to stumble. The upholstery on some of the furniture also was in poor condition. Mrs. Edgar and members of IEMA cooperated to raise the funds needed for new carpeting, drapes, and upholstery. In addition to those improvements, two hundred place settings of china were purchased, and the historically inaccurate carpeting that plagued the Lincoln bedroom was removed and the hardwood floors underneath restored. With the help of sponsor Marshall Field, Mrs. Edgar also created the memorable Hall of First Ladies, a portrait gallery of her predecessors that hangs in the south hallway of the Mansion.[20]

One of Mrs. Edgar's initiatives as first lady was a portrait gallery of her predecessors. Here she examines her handiwork.

Photo courtesy of Governor and Mrs. Edgar.

Mrs. Edgar's enjoys a moment with her precocious grandson Dakota.

Photo courtesy of Governor and Mrs. Edgar.

After moving into the Mansion, Mrs. Edgar recalled tiptoeing around and wondering if she could go into some of the rooms. She had enormous respect for the Mansion and its history, and she was in awe of the antiques, treasures, and of the historic personages, including Abraham Lincoln, who had visited the building. Mrs. Edgar was careful and frugal with the Mansion's expenses at a time of budget austerity for the state government. She even vacuumed the offices and swept the stoop, though the staff would quickly remind her that they were supposed to perform these chores. Governor Edgar recalled that soon after they moved into the Mansion, Elizabeth expressed an interest in having macaroni and cheese for dinner. A staff member overheard her remark, and the macaroni and cheese duly appeared at supper. In anticipation of similar requests, the cook purchased several cases of macaroni and cheese and stockpiled them in the kitchen. "You have to watch what you say in the Mansion," Governor Edgar chuckled. "I don't think Elizabeth asked for macaroni and cheese again for eighteen months and we had boxes of it!" When the press reviewed the Mansion's expenses, searching for luxury items like

The Edgars loved the beautiful walnut-paneled library. Here they celebrate their twenty-ninth wedding anniversary.

Photo courtesy of Governor and Mrs. Edgar.

Governor Edgar talks with Lieutenant Governor Bob Kustra in the Library

Photo courtesy of Governor and Mrs. Edgar.

lobster tails for which they had pilloried Governor Thompson, they instead discovered the macaroni and cheese. Edgar was amused by the resulting news accounts that portrayed his Mansion spending as frugal to the point of self-denial.[21]

For the Edgars, life at the Mansion sparkled with a cheering domesticity. Governor Edgar, a great dog-lover, delighted in walks to the Capitol with his golden retrievers Emy and Daisy. He enjoyed lunch on the east patio and took pleasure in menu planning. Mrs. Edgar might relax with some evening television viewing in the family room off the kitchen. Grandson Dakota, an engaging and active toddler, would visit and break into staff meetings with cookies in both hands, leaving the governor speechless with mirth. The family attended the Central Baptist Church across the street from the Mansion. Both of the Edgars tried to keep fit with regular exercise, the governor particularly so in the wake of his heart-related health problems. After open-heart surgery, Edgar worked out of the Mansion for two weeks while recovering.[22]

Brad Edgar and his bride Stacey Nehring cut the wedding cake at their Mansion reception, June 1994.

Photo courtesy of Governor and Mrs. Edgar.

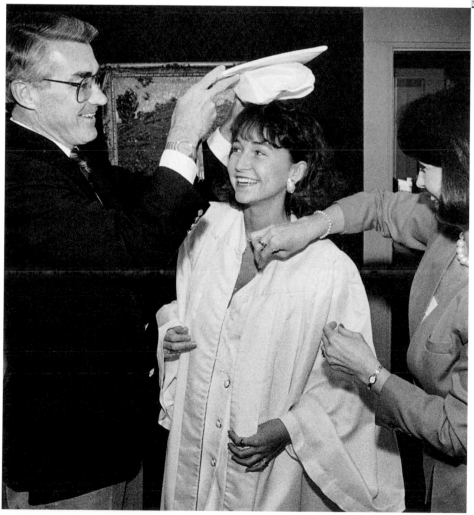

Proud parents, Jim and Brenda Edgar, with daughter Elizabeth on her graduation from Glenwood High School.

Photo courtesy of Governor and Mrs. Edgar.

Each year the governor and Mrs. Edgar hosted Fourth of July and Christmas parties for their staff, and there were special family events as well in the Mansion. Elizabeth held a pre-prom party for friends from Glenwood High School. When son Brad married Stacey Nehring in June 1994, a buffet supper was served in the public rooms, while a piano player serenaded the guests. Brad's daughter Cali Ann was baptized in a ceremony performed in the west public rooms. Celebrity guests at the Mansion included Olympic champion Bonnie Blair, Chicago Bears great Mike Singletary, prison outreach leader Chuck Colson, and radio personality Bob Collins.[23]

Living room of the private quarters. The walls were wallpapered to look like faux drapes of fine fabric.

Endnotes

1 [Illinois State Journal], Jan. 10, 1973, in Illinois Executive Mansion Restoration, ISHL.

2 Chicago Daily News, Nov. 13, 1973, in Illinois Executive Mansion Restoration, ISHL.

3 State Journal Register, Jan. 21, 1973, IEMA newsletter, May 23, 1973, Illinois Executive Mansion Restoration, ISHL.

4 Margaret Van Meter to Mrs. Walker, Springfield, Dec. 9, 1972, ISHL. IEMA minutes, Apr. 20, 1976, Illinois Executive Mansion Restoration, ISHL.

5 Lowell E. Anderson to Jane, Springfield, Apr. 3, 1973, State Journal Register, May 27, 1973, Aug. 24, 1975, IEMA newsletter, May 23, 1973, Nov. 22, 1974, Illinois Executive Mansion Restoration, ISHL.

6 Chicago Daily News, Mar. 4, 1974, Chicago Sun-Times, Mar. 4, 1974, Illinois Executive Mansion Restoration, ISHL.

7 IEMA annual meeting, Oct. 22, 1975, IEMA minutes, Mar. 31, 1976, IEMA meeting, Apr. 21, 1975, Illinois Executive Mansion Restoration, ISHL.

8 IEMA annual meeting, Oct. 22, 1975, Illinois Executive Mansion Restoration, ISHL.

9 IEMA newsletter, Sep. 7, 1976, SIU-E press release, Aug. 3, 1976, undated articles on same from unknown newspapers, William K. Alderfer, State Historian, to John L. Gilbert, General Counsel, SIU-E, Springfield, Nov. 21, 1980, Illinois Executive Mansion Restoration, ISHL.

10 Robert P. Howard, Mostly Good and Competent Men, 2nd ed. (1988; Springfield: University of Illinois at Springfield, 1999), 312-15.

11 Bloomington Pantagraph, June 19, 1977, Illinois Executive Mansion Restoration, ISHL.

12 Ibid. Chicago Sun Times, Feb. 20, 1977, State Journal-Register, Mar. 13, 1977, Illinois Executive Mansion Restoration, ISHL.

13 Lincoln Courier, Apr. 10, 1978, Alton Telegraph, Apr. 8, 1978, State Journal-Register, Apr. 27, May 20, 1978, Illinois Executive Mansion Restoration, ISHL.

14 IEMA newsletter, Feb. 9, 1978, Chicago Sun-Times, July 7, 1977, Lerner Skyline Newspapers week of Mar. 9, 1978, Invitation to de la Renta event, Feb. 22, 1978, IEMA statement of cash receipts and disbursements, July 30, 1979-Dec. 31, 1979, Jan. 1, 1980-Dec. 31, 1980, Rockford Morning Star, Sep. 19, 1977, Apr. 29, 1978, Illinois Executive Mansion Restoration, ISHL.

15 IEMA, statement of cash receipts and disbursements, Mar. 31, 1980-June 30, 1980, audited financial statements, Dec. 31, 1980-82. "Success at auction 'suite' to Thompson," State Journal-Register, June 18, 1980, The Official Opening of the Governor John P. Altgeld Suite, Executive Mansion, Dec. 20, 1980, Campanile Galleries, Inc., May 9, 1980, Illinois Executive Mansion Restoration, ISHL.

16 State Journal Register, Aug. 4, 1978, Thompson vertical file, ISHL.

17 State Journal-Register, Sep. 17, 1999. Lura Lynn Ryan, interview with author, May 28, 2002.

18 Howard, 328-29.

19 Tom Schafer, Meeting the Challenge: The Edgar Administration, 1991-1999 (Jim Edgar, 1998), 141-151.

20 Schafer, 151. Brenda Edgar, interview with author, Apr. 9, 2002.

21 Brenda Edgar interview, Apr. 9, 2002. Jim Edgar, interview with author, Apr. 17, 2002.

22 Brenda Edgar interview, Apr. 9, 2002. Jim Edgar interview, Apr. 17, 2002.

23 Brenda Edgar interview, Apr. 9, 2002. Jim Edgar interview, Apr. 17, 2002.

Chapter 9

East side of Mansion.

The beautiful elliptical staircase was re-created during Governor Ogilvie's term.

The Executive Mansion at the Turn of a New Century

George H. Ryan of Kankakee took the oath of office on January 11, 1999, as one of the longest tenured public officials in state history. With more than thirty years in government, Governor Ryan served as a county board member, state representative, speaker of the Illinois House, lieutenant governor, and secretary of state. Throughout his career, George Ryan's commanding physical presence and powerful baritone voice led many to describe him as "gruff" and hard to approach. But in reality, his public personae hid a soft-spoken man with a ready wit and quick smile; a committed family man who always placed the well being of others first.

Within hours of his inauguration, Governor Ryan and the first lady, Lura Lynn Ryan, opened their new home, the Executive Mansion, to a wide variety of visitors. In subsequent years, the Ryans used almost every public room and space on the grounds at one time or another to entertain state guests and conduct government business. "This is the people's house," Mrs. Ryan said. "We try to accommodate everyone who comes for a visit."

Sometimes, business and pleasure became intertwined. During a state reception at the Mansion in 2000, Governor Ryan's director of the state Department of Human Services, Linda Renee Baker, casually announced that she was engaged to be married. As the governor conveyed his congratulations, he asked where the ceremony was going to be held. Baker said she and her fiancée, Ron Roby, were having trouble finding a church. "Why don't you have it here," the governor said with a wave of his hand. And on June 8, 2001, Governor Ryan took the place of Baker's deceased father and "gave her away" in the south room, the first wedding held at the Mansion in more than a generation.

Author's note: *This chapter was written by Dave Urbanek and Susan Cavanaugh with Dan Monroe.*

The single term of the Ryan Administration was noted for an emphasis on improving education, reforming criminal justice, rebuilding the state's aging infrastructure, expanding the economy with bold overtures to new markets, and controlling the growth of government.

Many times, the governor's policies and proposals struck a less-than-popular chord with the public, even though in the end his accomplishments did improve the quality of life in Illinois. The governor's ability to communicate his message and to convince legislators, business and labor leaders, and average citizens of the merit of his ideas were the key to many victories in the General Assembly on behalf of Illinois citizens. Many times, the governor used the majesty of the Mansion's state rooms and the intimacy of the library, the ground floor dining room and grounds, as a stage where he could make his case and persuade others to support his positions.

Horticulturist Tom Martin tends to the beautiful flowers on the Mansion grounds.

Photo courtesy of Governor and Mrs. Ryan.

The governor first used the Mansion in this way during a series of receptions designed to generate support for his ambitious and historic Illinois FIRST program.

Within six months of his inauguration, Governor Ryan proposed and won legislative approval for Illinois FIRST, a five-year, $12 billion infrastructure improvement program that became emblematic of his term. Illinois FIRST eventually spawned more than 10,000 construction projects spread among all 102 Illinois counties, creating $7 billion in wages for working men and women.

Illinois FIRST sparked some controversy because its funding mechanism required the governor and legislators to raise a few fees that had not been altered in more than two decades. Nonetheless, the public embraced the program. Illinois FIRST led to the construction of more than 300 new schools; hundreds of miles of new or improved roads and bridges; new sewer systems; new fire trucks and rescue equipment; new mass transit buses and trains; better playgrounds and parks; 1,400 miles of biking trails and new libraries.

The governor used the Mansion to help change history in the summer of 1999 when he hosted a state dinner in honor of the highest ranking diplomat from Cuba in the

United States, Ambassador Fernando Remirez de Estenoz. During this dinner, which featured Illinois wines and Cuban cigars, Governor Ryan and Ambassador Remirez announced that the governor would travel to Cuba that fall on an historic humanitarian mission to deliver educational, medical, and agricultural products to the people of Cuba. That dinner, and subsequent dinners and meetings between the governor and Cuban officials at the Mansion, helped change forever the relationship between the United States and Cuba, as well as how the people of the two countries view each other.

In October of 1999, Governor Ryan became the first United States governor to visit Fidel Castro's communist stronghold in forty years. He led a delegation of 100 government officials, businessmen, doctors, farmers, educators, and media on a ten-day tour of farms, hospitals, schools, and historic sites, breaking down one of the last vestiges of the Cold War. The governor dined with Castro and broke new ground for other governors looking to sell their state's products to Cuba. While this trip generated protests from some quarters of the Cuban-American community, it nonetheless secured the governor's place with others as a bold leader at the forefront of a new relationship between the United States and Cuba. In 2001, Governor Ryan helped launch the first shipment of U.S. grain to Cuba in more than forty years – 24,000 metric tons of Illinois corn.

Governor George H. Ryan and Ambassador Fernando Remirez de Estenoz, Principal Officer of the Cuban Interests Section.

Photo courtesy of Governor and Mrs. Ryan.

Governor Ryan also found the Mansion an excellent place to quietly contemplate and wrestle with many of the great issues that came before him – such as the future of the death penalty in Illinois. Early in his term, Governor Ryan struggled personally for several weeks over whether to permit the execution of a convicted "ritual killer" who preyed on young women in the Chicago suburbs. After reviewing the case file and meeting with experts and staff members at the Mansion, the governor consented to the execution as justice served. Nonetheless, the awesome weight of the responsibility held by one man – any governor – over life and death, changed forever George Ryan's personal views on the death penalty.

Governor George H. Ryan, Mrs. Ryan, and her sister, Patti (Lowe) Lewis on the spacious porch of the Mansion.

Photo courtesy of Governor and Mrs. Ryan.

This change, coupled with a series of court decisions that freed thirteen innocent men from Illinois' death row – more than had been executed since 1977 – and ground-breaking research by Northwestern University students, prompted the governor to declare an historic, first-in-the-nation moratorium on the death penalty. Predictably, Governor Ryan's moratorium drew both protest and praise. The governor was honored by Amnesty International and other groups for a courageous stand that flew in the face of "conventional" political wisdom that political leaders must be "tough on crime." To George Ryan, however, fairness in the criminal justice system was not incompatible with punishing the guilty – and just as important.

With the pressures of office, George and Lura Lynn Ryan found the Mansion to be a refuge from the constant clamor of political life and the endless decisions of government. The guest rooms were often full with family and friends, and Mrs. Ryan often joked that on some family weekends there was an endless line-up of sleeping bags on the floor of the attic recreation room for their grandchildren and their friends. The Ryans have six children, five daughters and one son, including triplet daughters. That ensured that any Ryan home – in Kankakee or Springfield – was always busy and active.

The Ryan family.
Photo courtesy of Governor and Mrs. Ryan.

The couple hosted family reunion weekends and their high school class reunions on the grounds and graciously permitted friends and staff to host private parties on the grounds, providing they paid the bill. It was not unusual to hear the laughter of the Ryans' young grandchildren throughout the halls at any time, using walkie-talkies to stay in contact with their parents and grandparents. The governor often enjoyed playing catch or croquet with his grandchildren on the lawn.

When in Springfield, the governor and first lady typically took their meals at the Mansion in the ground floor dining room, but often on TV trays in front of the television in either the first-floor sitting room or the living room of their personal quarters. The governor was fond of entertaining dinner guests in the library with a roaring fire in the fireplace, reserving the south room and the dining room for

One of the happiest and most enduring couples in Illinois politics, George and Lura Lynn Ryan.

Photo courtesy of Governor and Mrs. Ryan.

larger groups. He was even known to preside occasionally in the kitchen, serving up bowls of his own home-made soup at a large table near the stove.

The Ryans' typical ritual after a state occasion included relaxing informally with guests over after-dinner drinks, coffee and cigars, trading political war stories, delving into the backgrounds of visitors, and often a tour of the Mansion by the home's curator or a volunteer guide.

The patio on the east side of the Mansion was used extensively by the Ryans to entertain, to relax, and as a quiet place to study reviews of legislation and other papers. The governor enjoyed informal lunches on the patio, as well as the use of an outdoor fireplace to break the chill of an evening.

In a tradition revived during the Ryan years, the governor hosted an annual "end-of-session" party on the grounds at the conclusion of each spring's legislative session. Lawmakers, officials, staff, media, lobbyists, and their guests crowded the lawns and driveways near the carriage house, where donated beverages and picnic food were served to all. The governor often indulged his guests with his fondness for Dixieland jazz, with small combos playing from a balcony to the guests below. These annual fetes often lasted until the wee hours of the morning, with lawmakers moving inside the Mansion to make use of the grand piano for sing-a-longs.

These annual parties were joined on the Ryans' calendar by festivals and parties honoring various ethnic groups, labor unions, business groups, historical societies, and charitable organizations. At the end of October, the children of Springfield would line up along the driveway for a chance to trick-or-treat at the Mansion – and to be greeted by a first lady dressed as a fairy godmother.

The Christmas season in the Ryans' home was a glorious tribute to holidays of the past, with decorated trees and miles of evergreen, holly, ivy, and ribbon decorating the doors, walls, fireplaces, and staircases.

Opening their home – the Mansion – to family, friends, and guests throughout the years was an old habit for the Ryans. Before his election as governor, the couple often hosted parties and dinners at their residences in Springfield or Kankakee as well as his State Capitol offices. But between 1999 and 2003, their home at Fourth and Jackson in Springfield became the ultimate extension of their hospitality.

George and Lura Lynn Ryan were married on June 10, 1956, and returned to Kankakee following the future governor's graduation from Ferris State College in Big Rapids, Michigan. The pair had met as freshmen at Kankakee High School, where the Governor played football and the first lady took to the stage. "George and I were high school sweethearts," Mrs. Ryan recalled. "I still remember what it was like to be newly in love and full of excitement for the future – because I still feel that way. Life is a journey, and I was lucky enough to find a wonderful partner."

Like his father and brother, Governor Ryan became a pharmacist and joined the family's small chain of drug stores in Kankakee. It was his interaction with the public as a businessman that led George Ryan into politics and, eventually, elective office. Lura Lynn Ryan was raised on a farm near Aroma Park in Kankakee County, skills that she used as first lady while competing in the Illinois State Fair's annual "Moo Moo Classic" cow milking contest. "When brought up in a rural community, you keep pretty active because people have to pull together to survive," Mrs. Ryan said. "When neighbors and others have problems, everyone helps."

Mrs. Ryan was raised in a rural community, where she performed farm chores such as milking a cow.

Photo courtesy of Governor and Mrs. Ryan.

Mrs. Ryan has been a tireless advocate for the prevention of substance abuse among young people.

Photo courtesy of Governor and Mrs. Ryan.

Together, the first lady's compassion for others and the governor's commitment to serving the public served them well in political life and helped their constituents deal with problems that government can solve. "What good is government if you don't use it to help people?" the governor once said.

Mrs. Ryan has been a staunch advocate for children, for substance abuse intervention and prevention programs, as well as early childhood education. "We didn't have the pressures that our children have today," Mrs. Ryan said. "We need mentoring from the extended family, the church, the community. Everybody has to pull together to be part of raising our children." Mrs. Ryan served on the board of directors of a number of charities in Illinois and was a strong supporter of Haymarket House in Chicago, a substance abuse treatment center. With her support, the governor, as lieutenant governor, led the establishment of the state's first independent agency specifically devoted to the treatment and prevention of substance abuse.

During the Ryan Administration, the first lady devoted much of her time to the creation and growth of "Futures for Kids," a statewide initiative designed to bring better coordination and greater awareness to what had been a jumble of initiatives targeting problems faced by young people. "Futures for Kids" was successful in launching and improving after school programs, drug abuse prevention, early childhood education, and parental involvement.

The first lady also championed greater awareness for Illinois' home-grown artists and craft artisans. The highly-successful Made in Illinois catalogue and artisans' exhibits at the Illinois State Fair did much to find new markets for painting, sculpture, needlework, and woodworking in Illinois. "We wanted to focus on the people who have these wonderful talents who work in their homes, but don't have a way to market their goods," she said.

Governor and Mrs. Ryan enjoy some light-hearted moments with children at the state fair.

Photo courtesy of Governor and Mrs. Ryan.

During the administration, Mrs. Ryan was highly active in the planning, construction, and development of the Abraham Lincoln Presidential Library and Museum in downtown Springfield. For years city leaders had discussed the concept of a "presidential library and museum" in Mr. Lincoln's hometown to bring focus to the already strong Lincoln experience in Central Illinois. But the concept remained just that until the Ryans threw their enthusiastic support and political will behind the project.

The library portion of the $115 million complex was completed before the end of the governor's term and now houses the three-million-item Illinois State Historical Library, one of the world's most important storehouses of information about Lincoln, his family, administration, and his times. While the governor busied himself with the construction of the complex, Mrs. Ryan became the founding chair of the Lincoln Presidential Library and Museum Foundation. The Foundation continues to raise funds for the operation of the site, as well as public and academic programs that enhance Lincoln's legacy and the study of public policy in Illinois and the United States.

One of the earliest fundraising drives for the Lincoln Library and Museum was the successful "Pennies for Lincoln" campaign. Based on a 1943 children's campaign that helped the state purchase a priceless copy of the Gettysburg Address in Lincoln's own hand, the 2000 "Pennies for Lincoln" effort raised $47,000 to help underwrite a new area of the museum devoted to interactive games and learning tools for young people.

Mrs. Ryan takes a telephone call at her desk in the Executive Mansion.

Photo courtesy of Governor and Mrs. Ryan.

Subsequent governors of Illinois and their families will find a revitalized and renewed Executive Mansion thanks to the Ryans. The couple devoted much to the refurbishment and upkeep of the home, as well as projects that enhanced the historical nature of the Mansion. The grounds were freshened and the house's fireplaces were unplugged and returned to their original wood-burning function. Chairs in the state dining room were replaced, and extensive repairs were made to the roof, the driveways, and to the exterior stairs that connect the house's sweeping verandas with the gardens. George and Lura Lynn Ryan's short four-year residence in the Executive Mansion will nonetheless be known as one of the most productive and busiest periods in the house's long history – a time when a handsome building shed years of quiet and formal stillness and flourished as a real family home.

The breakfast room in the private quarters

Following his stay at the Illinois Executive Mansion, Flat Stanley accompanied Governor and Mrs. Ryan to the White House to visit President and Mrs. George W. Bush.

Photo courtesy Governor and Mrs. Ryan.

Mrs Ryan has a word with George W. Bush during the 2000 presidential campaign.

Photo courtesy Governor and Mrs. Ryan.

Governor George H. Ryan and his wife Lura Lynn.
Photo courtesy of the Illinois State Historical Library.